Stadia Naming Rig

This book is an accessible, practical, and systematic guide to stadium naming rights sponsorship within sport, designed to help practitioners and students gain a better understanding of how naming rights work and the benefits that sport and corporate organisations may get from this kind of arrangement.

The book explains the key principles underpinning naming rights deals and sports sponsorship in non-specialist language for readers with little prior knowledge of the subject. Drawing on examples and case studies of naming rights sponsorships in international markets, across both professional and amateur sport, the book examines key practical issues such as how naming rights differ from other types of sponsorship, why brands should sign a naming rights deal, and how organisations can maximise their return on naming rights sponsorship.

Concise, informative, and practice-focused, this book offers essential insights for all sport management practitioners, for any marketing executives considering sport sponsorship, and for any students or researchers with an interest in sport marketing, sport management, marketing, or events and facilities management.

Leah Gillooly is Senior Lecturer in Marketing at Manchester Metropolitan University, UK. Her research interests include sports sponsorship, naming rights, branding, sports fan behaviour, and the sports customer experience. Leah regularly comments on sports marketing and sponsorship-related stories in the media.

Terry Eddy is Associate Professor of Sport Management at the University of Windsor, Canada. His primary research areas are sport sponsorship and consumer behaviour.

Dominic Medway is Professor of Marketing in the Institute of Place Management at Manchester Metropolitan University, UK. His research is primarily focused on the complex interactions between places, spaces, and those who manage and consume them, reflecting his academic training as a geographer.

Sport Business Insights
Series Editors
Aaron C.T. Smith, Loughborough University, UK
Constantino Stavros, RMIT University, Australia

Sport Business Insights is a series that aims to cut through the clutter, providing concise and relevant introductions to an array of contemporary topics related to the business of sport. Readers – including passionate practitioners, curious consumers and sport students alike – will discover direct and succinct volumes, carefully curated to present a useful blend of practice and theory. In a highly readable format, and prepared by leading experts, this series shines a spotlight on subjects of currency in sport business, offering a systematic guide to critical concepts and their practical application.
Available in this series:

Stadia Naming Rights in Sport

Leah Gillooly,
Terry Eddy and
Dominic Medway

Routledge
Taylor & Francis Group

LONDON AND NEW YORK

First published 2022
by Routledge
4 Park Square, Milton Park, Abingdon, Oxon OX14 4RN

and by Routledge
605 Third Avenue, New York, NY 10158

Routledge is an imprint of the Taylor & Francis Group, an informa business

British Library Cataloguing-in-Publication Data
A catalogue record for this book is available from the British Library

Library of Congress Cataloging-in-Publication Data
A catalog record has been requested for this book

ISBN: 978-0-367-63008-9 (hbk)
ISBN: 978-0-367-63010-2 (pbk)
ISBN: 978-1-003-11184-9 (ebk)

DOI: 10.4324/9781003111849

Typeset in Times New Roman
by codeMantra

Contents

Acknowledgements

We would like to extend our thanks to Zachary Evans, Ph.D. candidate, University of Windsor, for contributing some of the background research for the book.

1 Introducing Naming Rights Sponsorship

What is naming rights sponsorship?

Sponsorship has been defined as 'an investment in cash or in-kind, in an activity, in return for access to the exploitable commercial potential associated with that activity' (Meenaghan, 1991, p. 35). Naming rights can be seen as a particular type or form of sponsorship, which involves an exchange of money from a naming rights sponsor to the facility owner (known as the rights holder) in return for the right to name that facility or stadium. However, sponsorship agreements involving naming rights did not gain traction until after traditional sponsorship had become commonplace in sport. These types of deals have also previously been referred to as building/facility sponsorships or title sponsorships, but facility naming rights or stadia naming rights (followed, or not, by the word sponsorship) are the generally accepted terms. We will use the complete forms at times throughout this book, but will also frequently truncate to 'naming rights', which has become standard practice.

In addition to the differences in terminology, the way that naming rights fits within sponsorship paradigms is potentially changing. Naming rights have often been referred to as a special case of sponsorship or a distinct type of sponsorship. Historically, it made sense to categorise naming rights as a special case of traditional sponsorship, as facility naming sponsors rarely employed strategies beyond static signage to communicate their sponsorships (Fullerton & Merz, 2008). This is no longer the case, however, as the majority of brands purchasing naming rights now also activate their sponsorships in numerous other ways. The facility name tends to be the most widely visible piece of sponsorship agreements that frequently have many layers to connect with consumers in different ways (as we will discuss in Chapter 3). The question of how naming rights sponsorship is best conceived moving

DOI: 10.4324/9781003111849-1

forwards is something to which we will return in Chapter 6 when we look at the future of naming rights sponsorship in sport.

Regardless of how the term naming rights is defined, there are several aspects of such activity that are unique and/or notable compared to other forms of sponsorship/activation. First and most importantly, naming rights sponsors enjoy ubiquitous visibility compared to other sponsors (Fullerton & Merz, 2008). Whereas most sponsorship agreements (with the slight exception of shirt sponsors) tend to be noticed primarily (even exclusively) by teams' fans and/or attendees, naming rights sponsors are recognisable to much wider populations of sports fans nationally, or even internationally. Further, naming rights are arguably the most effective means of generating awareness beyond the sport in question, for example, with residents of, and visitors to, a region, or with anyone attending non-sporting events at a given facility. Second, naming rights agreements typically feature greater sums of money over longer periods of time than those sponsorships without naming rights. Naming rights agreements are typically signed for at least five years and can be in excess of 20 years. There are even a few examples of naming rights deals in perpetuity, such as the Carrier Dome at Syracuse University in the USA.[1] Finally, the name of a stadium is more than just an identifier – sports fans become attached to the places where their teams play, so stadia are often seen as a 'second home', and the name becomes part of the personality of the buildings.

It should be noted that the practice of selling naming rights extends to different areas within sport facilities as well. This has been especially popular in settings where organisations are concerned about changing decades-old names of historic stadia (e.g., US college sport). The most notable examples are sales of the names of the playing surface (e.g., Capital One Field at Maryland Stadium), which are seen as a compromise to completely eliminating the previous name of the facility. Naming deals also extend to other spaces within venues such as seating areas, club suites and boxes, food courts, and beer gardens. Even Madison Square Garden, self-proclaimed as the world's most famous arena and recognised as the last National Basketball Association (NBA) facility to bear a non-corporate name, contains numerous corporately-named spaces, including the J.P Morgan Club, the Delta Sky360 Club, and the Lexus Level Suites. Although these deals generate significant revenue for sport organisations, the totals are predictably much lower than for a facility deal, since the names are mainly only visible to event attendees (perhaps with occasional media mentions), and strong recognition may be limited to the relatively few attendees who experience those spaces first-hand. Given the difference in scope of the agreements, and numerous other nuances, we will not be covering these types of deals in this book.

We would also be remiss not to mention that, although sport facilities dominate the market for naming rights agreements, naming rights have become prevalent in several other industries, particularly for non-profit organisations. Theatres, amphitheatres, art galleries, and a host of other spaces frequently feature names purchased by corporations. These deals are often completed with many of the same objectives in mind as those seen with sports naming rights (e.g., raising the sponsor's awareness or enhancing their image). The main difference here is that the sponsoring brand is accessing very different target markets to sports fans or participants (e.g., art enthusiasts, concert goers, philanthropists). Obviously, this book is focused exclusively on sport; if readers are interested in learning more about the non-sport space, we suggest *Naming Rights: Legacy Gifts and Corporate Giving* (2008) by Terry Burton as a starting point.

A brief history

Although naming rights, as we know them, have only existed for about 50 years, there has been substantial growth and nuance in that time. Virtually every deal has offered something unique to the evolution of this sponsorship practice. Given that an exhaustive, detailed history is not our goal, we offer only an abridged version for the purpose of context.

The earliest examples of corporate names appearing on sports stadia came in the first half of the 20th century in the USA (e.g., Wrigley Field, Busch Stadium). However, these are generally not considered naming rights sponsorships per se because the brands and teams were both owned by the families of the same name, and no sponsorship exchange process was involved (Dodd, 2008). It seems that in most cases, there was some commercial intent behind these name choices, which may be why they are frequently mentioned in mainstream media as the first naming rights deals, but they do not qualify as sponsorships based on the widely accepted definitions that we are following in this book.

While there is substantial debate as to what the first true naming rights sponsorship was, we believe the first such deal occurred in 1971 when the Schaefer Brewing Company paid $150,000 to name the New England Patriots's stadium Schaefer Field (Noll & Zimbalist, 1997). The Schaefer name remained on the stadium until 1982. The second such deal came in 1973 when Rich Products, a frozen food supplier, paid $1.5 million over 20 years to name Rich Stadium, home of the National Football League's (NFL) Buffalo Bills (Crompton & Howard, 2003). The Rich Stadium deal more closely resembles the naming rights deals of today as it was the first to have a defined term for the agreement – this is perhaps why some cite the Rich deal as the first true stadium naming rights sponsorship.

Although the Schaefer and Rich deals were agreed within two years of each other, this idea of a corporation not affiliated with a given sports club paying to name its stadium did not take off for another 15–20 years. One reason appears to have been that the vast majority of the revenue required to run a sport franchise at that time could be covered by ticket sales. Further, at least within the USA, before the 1980s new facility construction costs were almost entirely covered by public funds. Thus, most organisations had little need for a naming rights partner, and instead named their stadia after prominent civic leaders (e.g., Hubert H. Humphrey Metrodome) or the local region (e.g., Louisiana Superdome) to acknowledge the public support.

As construction costs began to rise in the 1980s, public interest in funding new facilities with tax increases began to wane. Further, the introduction of free agency in North American professional sports in the late 1970s was substantially increasing the annual costs of running franchises. Thus, stadium/team owners began to seek new revenue streams to cover these costs, and the potential for naming rights could no longer be ignored (Nagel, 1999). The next major naming rights deal (after Rich Stadium) was signed in 1988, when the Los Angeles Forum became the Great Western Forum (Crompton & Howard, 2003), which served as a catalyst for naming rights throughout the rest of the 1980s and into the 1990s. By 2002, the market had exploded with almost 70% of professional sport venues in the USA having corporate naming rights sponsors, and the biggest deals ranging from $5–10 million per year (Crompton & Howard, 2003). From the mid-2000s onwards, naming rights continued to become the norm rather than the exception, with prices of up to $20 million per year starting to appear by 2006 (e.g., Citi Field in New York City).

During the late 1990s, naming rights sponsorships began to appear outside of the USA. One of the first deals came in the UK when Huddersfield Town Football Club's newly built stadium was named the Alfred McAlpine Stadium (Alfred McAlpine was the main construction partner for the new stadium and the naming rights were part of the deal to build the venue). The Alfred McAlpine Stadium is an example of the large number of new stadia built in the UK following the publication of the Taylor Report in 1990, which, in light of the 1989 Hillsborough Stadium disaster where a crush claimed the lives of 97[2] Liverpool Football Club fans, mandated UK football stadia to become all-seater. The naming rights market in the UK quickly escalated when, in 2004, Emirates Airlines agreed to pay 100 million pounds over 15 years to name Arsenal Football Club's new stadium in London, which was the largest per-year spend on a naming rights deal in the world at that time (Kemp, 2008).

Naming rights deals can now be found in approximately 40 countries worldwide. They have become commonplace in North America, much of Europe (particularly the UK, Germany, and Sweden), Japan, Australia, and New Zealand, and are emerging across the rest of the world (e.g., Brazil, China, and South Africa). In addition to spreading across the world, whenever it seems like naming rights prices are beginning to plateau, a new deal raises the bar. In 2017, Scotiabank set what was, at the time, a new naming rights record by signing a 20-year, $800 million CAD deal to rename Air Canada Centre in Toronto, home of the Toronto Raptors of the NBA and the Toronto Maple Leafs of the National Hockey League (NHL). Most recently, the cryptocurrency platform and exchange Crypto.com announced a 20-year, $700 million deal to rename the Staples Centre in Los Angeles to Crypto.com Arena. This deal may signal a new era in the scale of naming rights, as the Citi Field deal did in 2006, which we will discuss further in Chapter 6.

Trends and issues with naming rights

Sports sector diversification

Although the vast majority of early naming rights deals were in the realm of professional sport, naming rights have since spread to most other sports sectors. With continuing public funding constraints for sport and recreation across the globe, public sports facilities have turned to naming rights to fill the void. Many municipalities in North America have naming rights opportunities for facilities posted on their parks and recreation websites. For example, the County of San Diego, California offers naming rights for a majority of its recreation facilities, including ball fields and swimming pools. One notable example of a completed deal for a public sports complex came in 2017 when the City of Windsor, Ontario, Canada sold the naming rights for the former South Windsor Recreation Complex to Capri Pizzeria, a regional chain. The ten-year deal raised $160,000 CAD for various upgrades to the facility. In addition to the venue name, Capri Pizzeria obtained the rights for external signage and a concession stand.

Sponsors have also sought opportunities within youth/interscholastic sport, evident in the fact that schools have begun to engage in naming rights sponsorships. One of the first high school facility naming deals came in 2002 in Midland, Texas, USA, when Grande Communications purchased naming rights to the shared Midland High School/Robert E. Lee High School American football stadium (seating capacity of 15,000) for $1.2 million over 25 years. Other more recent high school deals in Texas have seen the per-year spends increase to $250,000–$300,000. Although the popularity of high school sport (particularly American football) in Texas is notable, leading to the higher than usual naming valuations, schools in other US states have also been able to secure six-figure deals.

US college sport, on the other hand, has seen naming rights deals emerge at a much slower pace compared to most other sport sectors, despite its unparalleled popularity and commercial potential compared to intercollegiate athletics in other countries. Although the Carrier Dome deal at Syracuse University has existed since 1979, corporate naming rights for college sport facilities are still the exception rather than the norm. Although there have been a few success stories (e.g., TCF Bank Stadium at the University of Minnesota), the names of major college sport facilities still typically fall within one of the following categories: (1) regional or institutional identifiers (e.g., Michigan Stadium at the University of Michigan), (2) memorials (e.g., Memorial Stadium at the University of Nebraska), or (3) notable alumni and/or donors (e.g., Boone Pickens Stadium at Oklahoma State University). As with other sporting contexts across the globe (e.g., European football), tradition is central to college sport fandom and, given that players can only compete for at most four years, the stadia (many of which are more than half a century old) are key elements of that tradition. Thus, many universities have been hesitant to explore naming rights, and there are still only a handful of deals across the college sport landscape. In these instances, many institutions have compromised by naming the field rather than the entire stadium (e.g., Alaska Airlines Field at Husky Stadium). Since research has specifically examined fan reactions to naming rights in the US collegiate sport context, we will revisit this in Chapter 4.

Types of sponsoring brands

In general, the naming rights space is dominated by large, global brands. This is no surprise given the sums required for the naming rights of major stadia at the most commercialised and highly visible levels of sport. Perhaps more interestingly, large brands are also omnipresent in smaller, less internationally visible sports sectors. For example, Coca-Cola, one of the 50 largest corporations in the world, currently holds only two naming rights sponsorships, and both are for venues housing teams in the minor league levels of professional sport in North America (Coca-Cola Coliseum in Toronto, Ontario, Canada and Coca-Cola Park in Allentown, Pennsylvania, USA). Similarly, Toyota currently has seven naming rights deals across the USA, and only one is for a facility home to a big four professional league team (Toyota Center in Houston, Texas). Even for these large, international brands, they have still seen value in smaller facilities that only offer regional visibility, for a number of different strategic reasons that we will discuss later in the book.

Although most major industry sectors are represented in naming rights sponsorships across the globe (particularly financials, energy, consumer staples, consumer discretionary, industrials, and technology), financial institutions (e.g., banks, credit unions, insurance companies, and asset managers) have generally been the most active and prevalent group of brands. Banks, in particular, have been leaders in naming rights since the beginning with Great Western Bank in Los Angeles (mentioned previously), while both Citibank and Scotiabank set new records for the size of their deals in 2006 and 2017, respectively. We can see more small- and medium-sized brands in this sector engaging in naming rights as well (e.g., Dort Federal Credit Union Event Center in Flint, Michigan, USA; Jyske Bank Boxen in Herning, Denmark; St. Galler Kantonalbank Arena in Rapperswil, Switzerland). The similarities in the products offered between banking institutions, and the fact that the differences between financial brands may be unclear to the general public, could be the reason why so many financial institutions seek naming rights to stand out from their competitors and gain long-term brand awareness in key markets.

Among consumer products, the most notable sector is automotive brands. The top five largest passenger car companies in the world (Toyota, Volkswagen, Daimler, Ford, and Honda) all have at least one naming rights deal within their brand families and are joined by numerous other global brands (e.g., Nissan, Mazda, and Kia). Almost as active as Toyota, mentioned above, is Volkswagen, which has six naming rights sponsorships globally, with four in Germany alone, across three of its brands (Audi Sportpark in Ingolstadt, Porsche-Arena in Stuttgart, Volkswagen Arena in Wolfsburg, and Volkswagen Halle in

Braunschweig). Mercedes-Benz and Cadillac also have the only two major naming rights deals for arenas in China, a market that remains somewhat untapped.

On the other hand, airlines were major players in the early days of naming rights, but as that industry has declined globally over the past decade, so has the number of facility names associated with airlines. Several prominent global brands have had major naming rights deals in the past that they have not renewed (e.g., American Airlines Arena in Miami, Florida, USA, and Etihad Stadium in Melbourne, Australia). Further, few new deals have emerged in the past decade from this sector.

It seems likely that the most growth in the future may come from the technology sector, although these companies are currently underrepresented in the naming rights space, especially given their size and significance in the global economy. The explosion of the technology sector in the late 1990s brought several naming partners (e.g., CMGI and PSINet), but with the tech bubble collapse in the early 2000s, these deals went with the demise of those companies. Telecommunications companies have been active in naming rights since the beginning, and currently have deals for major sport facilities in numerous countries around the world (e.g., Orange Velodrome in Marseille, France; Optus Stadium in Perth, Australia; Turk Telekom Stadium in Istanbul, Turkey).

Buy local

Up until the early 2000s, approximately 80% of naming rights deals were between sport facilities and brands that were based in the same region (Lefton, 2009). One of the first, and still most prominent, brands that began this trend was Target, a Fortune 500 retailer based in Minneapolis, Minnesota, USA. They have held naming rights to the Target Center, home of the Minnesota Timberwolves of the NBA, since 1990. They also purchased the name to Target Field, home of Major League Baseball's (MLB) Minnesota Twins, in 2010, which is virtually next door to the Target Center. Other notable examples include American Airlines Center in Dallas, Texas, USA; Nissan Stadium in Yokohama, Japan; Rogers Centre in Toronto, Ontario, Canada; and Menora Mivtachim Arena in Tel Aviv, Israel. These major brands are most likely seeking to maximise the effect of higher local recognition rates, and also perhaps hoping to be perceived as 'giving back' to the communities where they are based.

Although the naming rights landscape is dominated by major brands, as discussed previously, there are occasions where smaller companies have entered into naming deals, often due (at least in part) to being locally based. For example, Air Creebec, a small regional airline owned entirely by the Cree people based in Val-d'Or, Quebec, Canada – a small, isolated, northern community – purchased naming rights to the Centre Air Creebec. The arena houses the Val-d'Or Foreurs of the Canadian Hockey League (CHL), who compete primarily against teams across Quebec and Atlantic Canada. Thus, the sponsor enjoys increased visibility across its region, as well as embedding itself in the local community. Although examples like these abound in smaller markets, and/or for less prominent facilities, there are times when small brands have been able to secure major deals. One of the first such examples came during the tech boom of the late 1990s, when 3com purchased the name of historic Candlestick Park in San Francisco, California, USA. Although the agreement was met with anger by fans, the deal brought immense recognition to 3com, which was an upstart brand at the time located in the San Francisco area (and survived the tech bubble collapse, eventually being bought by Hewlett Packard).

While the 'buy local' trend is still common in naming rights, we have begun to see more naming rights deals from brands not based in the same region, or even country, as the sports facility. These deals often appear to be part of a penetration strategy for the new market/country. One of the first such examples was Emirates Stadium in London, mentioned previously. Since then, Toyota (based in Japan) and TD Bank (based in Canada) both have the majority of their multiple naming rights agreements in the USA, which is a primary growth market for both brands. In addition, companies may use a broader geographic approach to naming rights to establish themselves as global brands. The most globally diversified naming rights sponsor is Allianz, which owns naming rights to Allianz Arena, the most prominent stadium in its home market of Munich, Germany, but also has deals in Australia, Austria, Brazil, France, Italy, and the USA. This will be an interesting trend to track as the world economy continues to globalise, which we will discuss further in Chapter 6.

Controversy

Naming rights sponsorships have been rife with controversy since the beginning. For example, the 1988 naming agreement for the Great

Western Forum venue discussed above was not immediately embraced by citizens of Los Angeles. However, by that time the Los Angeles Lakers had become one of the greatest NBA teams of all time, and the Los Angeles Kings of the NHL had recently signed Wayne Gretzky (nicknamed 'the Great One'). This, in addition to Los Angeles being in the Western USA, made the name sound fairly natural in many ways; thus, the name did eventually gain some acceptance, though many fans still called it 'the Forum'. More of these fan reactions, particularly to the renaming of stadia that did not initially carry corporate names, will be covered in Chapter 4.

Up until 2001, sports organisations were mainly concerned with whether or not their naming partner was financially stable, and little consideration was given to the sponsor's ethics or business practices, and the potential legal issues that could follow. This changed after Enron purchased the rights to Enron Field, the new home of the Houston Astros of MLB in 1999. The energy company became embroiled in scandal in the early 2000s due to bankruptcy and corporate fraud, which had a damaging spillover effect on the Astros in the form of a public and media backlash with associated negative perceptions. Due to lack of provisions in the contract for such an event, the Astros had to pay Enron $2.1 million to be released from the agreement (Jensen & Butler, 2007). Since this time, greater scrutiny has been placed on potential sponsors by sport organisations, but there are still occasions when controversial sponsors have been able to work their way towards naming rights agreements (e.g., GEO Group at Florida Atlantic University; Bishop, 2013). We will discuss these types of cases in more detail in Chapter 4, in relation to fan reactions.

An ethical issue that has begun to be raised more frequently by fans and/or media is incongruence between the naming sponsor and sports organisation, often based on the nature of the sponsor's business or corporate mission/values. For example, Budweiser Gardens in London, Ontario, Canada houses the London Knights of the CHL as its primary tenant, despite many players in that league being below the legal drinking age of 19 (some as young as 15). Similarly, the Yuengling[3] Center houses teams from the University of South Florida in Tampa, Florida, USA, where most of the student athletes (and student attendees) are below the legal drinking age of 21. Another controversial product sector is gambling, with an increasing number of brands in this sector involved in sponsorship of sport. While in many markets gambling is synonymous with sport, concerns have been raised as to its wider and more negative societal impacts, which may shape perceptions of sponsorships by such brands. There has been little penetration of the naming rights market by this sector to date, although the Tip-sport Arena in Prague, Czech Republic and the Bet365 Stadium in Stoke-on-Trent, UK are notable exceptions.

Outline for the book

This chapter has offered the reader background knowledge, history, and trends in naming rights to begin to understand the current global marketplace for these sponsorships. Going forward, we will focus on issues and considerations that are necessary and important to more fully understand naming rights in sport. Chapter 2 offers a more in-depth discussion of how naming rights work; specifically, why sponsors pursue naming rights and the benefits to all parties in the agreements. Chapter 3 then examines how brands activate their naming rights deals for success. In Chapter 4, we provide a thorough overview of the body of research on fan reactions to naming rights, noting the lessons that brands and sports organisations can learn from this work. Chapter 5 offers suggestions on decision making, in terms of the selling (or not) of naming rights and how to choose a naming rights partner. This will take the perspective of both sports organisations and potential sponsors. Finally, Chapter 6 concludes the book by continuing the discussion of trends from this chapter to look forward at the future of naming rights in sport.

Notes

1 In 1979, Carrier paid $2.75 million towards construction costs for the stadium and in return was granted naming rights in perpetuity. More recently, there has been speculation that Syracuse University might be looking for a way out of the deal, thus opening up opportunities for new naming rights deals which would bring in significant revenue (Carlson, 2019).
2 Ninety-four people died on 15 April 1989, the day of the match. Another person died in hospital several days later, and another in 1993. Then, 32 years later, in July 2021 Andrew Devine, who suffered irreversible brain injuries in the Hillsborough disaster, died. A coroner ruled that he was the 97th victim.
3 Yuengling is a US beer brand.

References

Bishop, G. (2013, February 19). *A Company That Runs Prisons Will Have Its Name on a Stadium.* https://www.nytimes.com/2013/02/20/sports/ncaafoot-ball/a-company-that-runs-prisons-will-have-its-name-on-a-stadium.htm-

l#:~:text=The%20GEO%20Group%2C%20which%20is, in%20Florida%20
Atlantic's%20athletic%20history

Carlson, C. (2019, October 3). *Why Is Syracuse Avoiding the Word Carrier?
Experts Say there's a Rhyme, Reason.* https://www.syracuse.com/orange-
basketball/2019/10/why-is-syracuse-avoiding-the-word-carrier-experts-
say-theres-a-rhyme-reason.html

Crompton, J., & Howard, D. (2003). The American experience with facility
naming rights: opportunities for English professional football teams. *Man-
aging Leisure, 8*(4), 212–226. https://doi.org/10.1080/1360671032000148585

Dodd, M. (2008, February 28). For some Cubs fans, renaming Wrigley is deal-
breaker. *USA Today*, 1C.

Fullerton, S., & Merz, G. R. (2008). The four domains of sports marketing: A
conceptual framework. *Sport Marketing Quarterly, 17*(2), 90–108.

Jensen, R., & Butler, B. (2007). Is sport becoming too commercialised?
The Houston Astros' public relations crisis. *International Journal of
Sports Marketing and Sponsorship, 9*(1), 23–32. https://doi.org/10.1108/
IJSMS-09-01-2007-B004

Kemp, E. (2008, January 22). *New stadiums offer brands naming rights
opportunities.* Campaign US. https://www.campaignlive.com/article/
new-stadiums-offer-brands-naming-rights-opportunities/778074

Lefton, T. (2009). TD Ameritrade titles new home of college WS. *Street &
Smith's Sportsbusiness Journal, 12*(8), 1.

Meenaghan, T. (1991). The role of sponsorship in the marketing communications mix. *International Journal of Advertising, 10*(1), 35–47. https://doi.org/
10.1080/02650487.1991.11104432

Nagel, M. S. (1999). *Recognition of corporate-named professional sports
facilities and the implications for future sponsorship agreements* (Doctoral
thesis, University of Northern Colorado). ProQuest Dissertations and
Theses Global https://www.proquest.com/dissertations-theses/recognition-
corporate-named-professional-sports/docview/304513305/
se-2?accountid=12507

Noll, R. G., & Zimbalist, A. (1997). Sports, jobs, and taxes. *Brookings Review,
15*(3), 35–40.

2 Why Do Brands Buy Naming Rights?

As with many different vehicles for sponsorship, stadia naming rights can be used by sponsors to achieve a wide range of objectives. This makes stadia naming rights a valuable and versatile marketing tool for brands both large and small. Using examples covering sponsors from different sectors and rights holders across a range of sports and markets, this chapter will outline the types of objectives most commonly pursued through stadia naming rights sponsorship and in doing so will explore how naming rights work to achieve these objectives for sponsors. The best naming rights sponsorships not only benefit the sponsor but also benefit other stakeholders. Sponsorship Consultant, Kim Skildum-Reid (2021) advocates that sponsorship should follow a principle of win-win-win, highlighting that sponsors, rights holders, and fans should all benefit from a sponsorship. When thinking about naming rights, thanks to the geographic position and role of stadia within their towns and cities, we can extend this to win-win-win-win, with the fourth beneficiary being local residents and communities. Therefore, the chapter will conclude with examples of how stadia naming rights can benefit stakeholders beyond the sponsor and rights holder, identifying areas of best practice to ensure that these wider stakeholders are considered from the start of naming rights negotiations and planning.

Objectives pursued through stadia naming rights sponsorship

When considering the objectives pursued by stadia naming rights sponsors, it is helpful for us to think about them in the context of the journey taken by consumers towards eventual purchase of a sponsor's products or services. The customer journey represents all of the different touchpoints or interactions someone has with a brand up to and

DOI: 10.4324/9781003111849-2

beyond the purchase of that organisation's product. One such touch-point can be exposure to sponsorship, such as stadium naming. From the brand side, a useful framework which represents the stages that consumers must be moved through from initially being unaware of the brand to purchasing products bearing its name (and beyond), is the buying funnel. The buying funnel therefore outlines the stages from initial consumer awareness of a brand, through consideration, pref-erence, and intention, to purchase, loyalty, and ultimately customer advocacy (Kotler et al., 2006).

Stadia naming rights sponsorship and brand awareness

At the top of the buying funnel is 'awareness'. It is at this stage where naming rights sponsorship can have a significant impact, increasing consumers' familiarity with a brand through frequent media men-tions and exposure. Unless people are aware of a brand, naming rights sponsors will not be able to achieve any other objectives because brand awareness is a pre-condition for the next stages in the buying funnel, such as consideration or preference. As outlined in Chapter 1, naming rights are a highly visible form of sponsorship, with the names of spon-sors emblazoned in large lettering across stadia frontages, concourses, and road signs. In addition, by acquiring the naming rights to a sta-dium, sponsors secure numerous media mentions of their brand name every time the stadium is referred to across television, radio, press, and online. Therefore, media exposure represents a commonly cited objective pursued by stadia naming rights sponsors. However, media exposure in itself can be considered an intermediate step towards the primary objective of increasing brand awareness.

One brand that has aggressively pursued the objective of brand awareness through sponsorship, including multiple stadia nam-ing rights deals, is Emirates. Securing the naming rights to English Premier League football club Arsenal's Emirates Stadium, and two English cricket grounds (Emirates Old Trafford in Manchester and Emirates Riverside in County Durham) has helped to grow aware-ness of the airline Emirates in the UK market. In the case of Arsenal's Emirates Stadium, the worldwide media coverage of the English Pre-mier League also contributes to growing Emirates's brand awareness internationally. While cricket has a lesser profile on the world stage, acquiring the naming rights to Emirates Old Trafford has allowed the brand to gain exposure beyond sport, as this is a venue used exten-sively for corporate functions and concerts as well as having an on-site hotel attracting both tourists and business travellers. Emirates is also the naming rights sponsor for Emirates Airline Park in Johannesburg,

South Africa, alongside an extensive portfolio of other sponsorships across sports including tennis, sailing, golf, motorsport, and horse racing. These are all motivated by a quest for the valuable exposure that is possible through the global reach and power of sport.

When measuring the outcomes of stadia naming rights, the focus is often on sponsorship awareness (which is clearly linked to, but not the same as, brand awareness). Sponsorship awareness can be broken into recall and recognition. Recall is where people are asked to name the sponsor of a particular stadium, and recognition is where people are given a list of brands and asked to identify which one is the sponsor of the stadium. The relative value of recall or recognition to a given brand varies according to a variety of reasons and factors, which are beyond the scope of this book. To find out more about sponsorship recall and recognition, see Lardinoit and Derbaix (2001). What we do know, is that people often struggle to name more than a handful of naming rights sponsors (Haan & Shank, 2004) when they are asked things such as: 'Which brands sponsor NFL stadia'? These kinds of questions are measuring sponsorship recall, which requires more mental processing on the part of consumers than recognition. This explains why sponsorship recognition scores are invariably higher than recall scores.

The exposure associated with stadia naming rights allows sponsors to reach a very wide audience, including fans of the team(s) playing at the sponsored stadium, fans of rival teams, and general sports fans as well as the broader public. All these audiences are likely to see and hear references to the stadium name on signage and through the media. However, by the very nature of the differing frequencies with which these different groups will be exposed to the stadium sponsor name, and the associated level of interest in any mental processing devoted to that information by these groups, we can reasonably conclude that recall of stadia naming rights sponsors is higher amongst relevant sports fans than the general public. Nevertheless, the familiarity with a brand that can be built up among the general public through repeated exposures to a sponsored stadium name can lead to a high level of sponsorship and brand recognition. For example, people living around the former Reebok Stadium in Bolton, UK (home to Bolton Wanderers Football Club and subsequently renamed Macron Stadium and the University of Bolton Stadium), which encompasses a retail and leisure park, often still identify the area as 'the Reebok'. In this regard, it is not uncommon to hear local residents saying 'we're going shopping up at the Reebok' (Gillooly et al., 2021), even years after the company in question ceased to be the naming rights sponsor of the stadium. This example highlights how the names of stadia, through their prominent role as landmarks within a town or city, percolate into wider discourses among the public. This extends the reach of naming rights sponsorship to more broadly impact awareness as part of the first stage of the buying funnel. It also highlights how sponsors can benefit from recognition and awareness even when their stadia naming rights deal ends. While fans who know a new stadium sponsor's name may be more likely to use it, the wider population for whom learning new stadia names is less important are likely to persist in the use of previous venue names out of habit (Light & Young, 2014). The persistence of former corporate stadia names can be seen as an advantage for former sponsors who continue to benefit from their naming rights deal for several years after it ends, but it can also become a threat to new naming rights sponsors who face the challenge of displacing the former stadium name in everyday speech. The answer of how to do this lies in successfully activating the sponsorship (see Chapter 3).

A range of other factors that impact the extent to which stadia naming rights sponsorship can build brand awareness have also been identified. In most cases, research has not specifically covered the context of stadia naming rights, but rather the sponsorship of events or teams. However, beyond achieving potentially wider levels of awareness through media mentions, as discussed above, there is nothing unique about stadia naming rights sponsorship that means the learnings from other sponsorship contexts will not hold true. One such factor is how well-known a stadium naming sponsor brand is, often referred to as prominence (Pham & Johar, 2001). Research suggests that well-known brands are identified as sponsors more frequently than lesser-known brands, giving big brands an advantage in the naming rights field. However, other research has suggested that sponsorship can be effective at building brand name awareness (if nothing else) even for new and less prominent brands (Donlan, 2013). In the case of well-known brands, the visibility associated with stadia naming rights sponsorship means they can use it to keep their brand at the top of people's minds through repeated exposures, while for less prominent brands, it can be used to stimulate that first awareness of the brand name. However, as will be discussed further in Chapter 3, to go beyond awareness, stadia naming rights sponsorship requires activation.

Naming rights sponsorship and brand consideration

Moving beyond awareness, the next two stages in the buying funnel are 'consideration' and 'preference'. At these stages, consumers start to learn more about a brand, acquiring information about its associated products or services. They may also move towards including the brand in the group they select from for their ultimate purchase, known as the consideration set. Relating this to stadia naming rights sponsorship, at these stages sponsors are pursuing objectives relating to brand image and brand attitudes/opinion. Here, the goal is to encourage consumers to think positively about the sponsor brand. Naming rights can also be a way of legitimising the brand, by indicating to potential customers the brand's status and intent and giving them a reason to include the new brand in their consideration set. While established brands may already possess a stock of brand associations in the minds of consumers, for new brands these are non-existent and so people may be wary of purchasing products bearing the brand's name. By engaging in a naming rights sponsorship, a new brand not only gains awareness (as discussed above), but the scale of the sponsorship investment can send signals to the customer, who may think: 'if they are big enough to sponsor Stadium X then they must be a secure bet for me to do business with'. To date, new brands have tended to use other sponsorship vehicles, such as shirt or event sponsorship as a means of achieving such benefits. For example, Cinch, an online platform for researching, buying, and selling cars in the UK was launched in 2019 and within two years had signed sponsorship deals with a range of sporting properties, including the Queen's Club Championships tennis event, the England and Wales Cricket Board, Premier League football team Tottenham Hotspur, the Scottish Professional Football League, and English rugby union team Northampton Saints. These sponsorships, combined with extensive advertising and other promotions, helped to establish Cinch in the minds of consumers looking to buy and sell cars, and led to significant sales growth in a very short space of time. While this example concerns other sponsorship vehicles, the current scale and visibility of naming rights sponsorship suggests that it has potential to deliver as much, if not more value for new brands looking to cement their position in consumers' brand consideration sets.

Legitimising a brand by virtue of association with a sports stadium is one aspect of building a brand's image. This brand image enhancement is important for naming rights sponsors who are both new and well-established. The impact of stadia naming rights sponsorship on brand image can be explained through the mechanism of brand image transfer, which is one of the key theoretical frameworks we can use to explain how sponsorship works. By acquiring the naming rights to a stadium, a sponsor brand becomes linked with the brand of the stadium and/or the team which plays there. Brand image transfer works on the principle that consumers infer that associations from the rights holder also hold true for the sponsor (i.e., the image of the rights holder is transferred to the sponsor). Therefore, by acquiring naming rights to a stadium, the sponsor 'borrows' the associations held by consumers about the venue, or more likely about the team which plays there, and transfers those onto their brand. Brand image transfer is underpinned by a body of theory from psychology, most notably associative network and schema theory – see Gwinner (1997) and Smith (2004) for a more detailed discussion of these theoretical underpinnings.

Building or enhancing brand image is a commonly pursued objective of naming rights sponsorship. An example of how naming rights sponsors consider the image and brand-building benefits of stadia sponsorship can be found with the Cbus Super Stadium in Queensland, Australia. This naming rights deal between Cbus, a superannuation fund provider for the construction industry, and Australian rugby league club the Gold Coast Titans allowed Cbus to grow its brand within the Gold Coast community. In announcing the deal, Cbus chairman Steve Bracks talked of the power of partnering with such an 'iconic ground' (Meyn, 2014), thus highlighting the positive associations with stadia that sponsors want to transfer onto their brands. As another example, clothing brand Levi Strauss & Co used its naming rights deal with NFL team the San Francisco 49ers (naming the team's new stadium Levi's Stadium) as a means of conveying the sports and cultural lifestyle associations of the team and its stadium onto the Levi's brand. This was part of an effort to revitalise the Levi's brand image amongst a customer segment that had drifted away. These examples highlight the power of sporting venues as properties with valuable sets of associations that sponsor brands want to borrow through their sponsorship pairing.

As with brand awareness, the extent to which naming rights sponsorships contribute to the transfer of brand image associations varies according to a range of factors. One particularly important variable is 'team identification', which refers to the extent to which someone feels attached to an object – in this case, a sports team and its stadium. Fans of a team can vary in their level of identification, from the casual spectator through to the most avid fan, while non-fans would exhibit little or no identification with a particular team (perhaps beyond a casual allegiance based on home town or place of residence). Research suggests that team identification positively impacts attitudes towards naming rights sponsorship (Chen & Zhang, 2012; Reysen et al., 2012). Therefore, we can conclude that the impact of naming rights sponsorship on brand attitudes and associations is likely to be stronger among fans of the sponsored stadium's team. That is not to say that brand consideration and preference cannot be built more widely through stadia naming rights sponsorships, but the effects are likely to be greater among fans as a result of the attachment they feel to the team. Another important factor which plays a significant role in the success of naming rights sponsorship for building positive brand associations is sponsorship fit, which refers to whether there is a logical connection between a sponsor brand and a rights holder. Sponsorship fit also plays an important role in shaping fans' reactions to stadia naming rights sponsorships, so we will discuss it fully in Chapter 4.

Naming rights sponsorship and sales

The buying funnel model progresses to the purchase stage, where a consumer decides to purchase a product or service from the brand in question. It is reasonable to assume, therefore, that a goal of many naming rights sponsorships is to drive sales. However, in this regard, there is currently limited evidence in academic studies of naming rights sponsorship's success. This is not to say that there is no evidence of sales impacts, just that this evidence is more limited than that supporting the effect of naming rights on intermediate measures such as awareness and brand image. One of the main reasons for this is the difficulty in measuring the direct drivers or causes of sales uplifts. Thus, we might best consider sales as an indirect goal of naming rights sponsorship, achieved as an aspirational consequence of the previously discussed objectives.

One of the main difficulties in identifying the impact of naming rights on sales is the challenge of how to isolate and measure the effect. It is unlikely that any brand will engage solely in stadia naming rights sponsorship and no other marketing activities. Therefore, separating out the impact of the naming rights from that of other marketing activities, including advertising, sales promotions, pricing, and distribution offers is problematic. Indeed, the very fact that naming rights sponsorship is just one of the many marketing tools employed by brands suggests that these have a synergistic impact, reinforcing each other and so teasing out exactly which sales were driven by which marketing tools would be almost impossible. It is these difficulties in measurement that have led most studies to focus on purchase intention rather than actual purchase.

There is some evidence that naming rights sponsorship can lead to increased purchase intention (Eddy, 2014), particularly from fans who hold positive attitudes towards sponsorship in sport. While there is not a perfect relationship between purchase intention and actual purchase, people's intentions do largely shape their ultimate behaviours. However, as will be discussed in Chapter 4, there are many factors which shape fans' attitudes towards stadia naming rights sponsors and these can have a profound impact on the extent to which fans would consider purchasing the products or services of their favourite team's stadium sponsor. These challenges, however, haven't stopped brands and rights holders from wanting to find out information on sales. For brands, the Finance Director (or equivalent) may well want firm evidence of the return on the naming rights investment, while this information would be highly prized by rights holders as it would help them in placing a value on the naming rights for their stadia.

Naming rights sponsorship and brand loyalty

Brands are rarely seeking one-off purchases from customers. Rather, they want to cultivate loyal, repeat-customers, who will be significantly more valuable in the long term (hence the customer loyalty and advocacy stages in the buying funnel). There has, so far, been limited research into the impact of sponsorship on brand loyalty and, at the time of writing, none in the context of naming rights. However, we can draw some interesting insights from studies of team and event sponsorship in relation to brand loyalty. These provide tentative evidence that sponsorship can help to build brand loyalty (Donlan, 2014), notably among fans who are highly identified with the team or event (Tsordia et al., 2018), or who view themselves as having a shared image with the sponsored property (Mazodier & Merunka, 2012; Sirgy et al., 2008). From this research, we might reasonably infer that naming rights sponsorship can have a positive impact on loyalty towards the sponsor brand, particularly for fans of the team that plays at the stadium.

It may also be the case that naming rights are, in fact, better than sponsorship of a one-off event for brands looking to build brand loyalty. Work on Olympic Games sponsorship found that the positive impact on brand loyalty was short-lived (Mazodier & Merunka, 2012). Therefore, the long duration of most naming rights agreements gives this form of sponsorship an advantage over one-off or irregular events. By keeping the brand in front of the consumer and displaying commitment to a long-term sponsorship relationship, naming rights sponsors can potentially benefit from increased brand loyalty across a number of years. Beyond the stages of the buying funnel, naming rights may also be used to pursue a range of other objectives. It is to these that we will now turn.

Naming rights sponsorship and corporate social responsibility

Corporate social responsibility (CSR) refers to the 'economic, legal, ethical and discretionary' expectations that society has of organisations (Carroll, 1979, p. 499). Increasingly, brands are expected to not only be good corporate citizens but to give something back to the communities within which they operate. Sport (and therefore the sponsorship of sport) has a number of characteristics that make it a suitable vehicle for brands to use when pursuing objectives relating to CSR. These include not only the positive health impacts of sport, but also the opportunities it provides for social interaction. Data suggested that, as of 2018, showcasing CSR was an important objective for 29% of brands involved in sports sponsorship (IEG, 2017). If done well, stadia naming rights sponsorship can provide brands with a useful opportunity to demonstrate their social commitment.

The way in which sponsorship is perceived by consumers is key to its ability to contribute to CSR objectives. While there is evidence that sponsorship of sport in and of itself can be useful as a CSR tool, a study by Woisetschläger et al. (2017) suggests that naming rights sponsorship is viewed as being motivated more by business reasons (e.g., potential sales and profits uplift) than a desire by organisations to be good corporate citizens. This, in turn, could harm the effectiveness of naming rights as a sponsorship tool for achieving CSR objectives. According to attribution theory, consumers will take a view on a brand's likely motives based on its actions. If a brand's actions are considered as being more altruistic than commercial, then consumers will respond more favourably towards that brand. In the context of stadia naming rights, it is often the case that sponsorship of local-, community-, and grassroots-level sport is viewed as being more altruistic. Therefore, brands seeking to pursue CSR-related objectives might consider sponsoring a community sports facility rather than a stadium used purely for elite sport. However, this does not always have to be the case, as illustrated by the examples below.

An interesting example of stadia naming rights sponsorship being used to achieve objectives relating to CSR is the Friends Arena in Solna, Sweden. The naming rights to this venue, which hosts football as well as music concerts, are owned by Swedbank. However, in 2012 Swedbank announced that the rights would be given over to the Friends Foundation, a not-for-profit organisation working to prevent bullying (Businesswire, 2012). Swedbank is a main sponsor of the Friends Foundation, so the naming rights sponsorship forms an extension of this partnership, and demonstrates the bank's engagement with society, specifically around support for young people. In this case, Swedbank does not gain from the exposure benefits traditionally associated with naming rights sponsorship, but it is using its naming rights as part of a wider, holistic sponsorship strategy focused around a company commitment to responsible business. While there are likely to be many reasons for the success of this sponsorship, the fact that Swedbank gave away its brand name visibility benefits signals to consumers a more altruistic motive. This goes beyond simply adding a CSR element into a conventional naming rights deal with Swedbank's own name up on the arena. In turn, consumers are likely to form more favourable attitudes towards Swedbank, allowing it to successfully use naming rights as part of its overall CSR-related sponsorship strategy. In a similar example, Amazon purchased the naming rights to a multi-purpose sports arena in Seattle, which has been called the Climate Pledge Arena. In this case, Amazon appears to be using its naming rights agreement to shine a spotlight on its broader sustainability goals, again eschewing the usual visibility benefits of naming rights sponsorship. The extent to which these two cases represent isolated examples or whether brands will begin to use naming rights sponsorships differently remains to be seen. This and several other future trends around naming rights sponsorship are explored more fully in Chapter 6.

Naming rights sponsorship and company value

Most of the objectives or benefits of stadia naming rights discussed so far have related to marketing outcomes. However, it is possible that signing a naming rights deal might impact on the share value of the sponsor, thus having a positive impact on overall company value. The extent to which naming rights sponsorship positively impacts company share prices is somewhat disputed. A number of academic studies have used a statistical technique called the event study methodology to calculate the impact of stadia naming rights deal announcements on the share price of the naming rights sponsor. This is done by creating a model of the share price returns that could normally be expected and deducting these from the returns actually achieved on the day of the announcement. The difference (what is referred to as abnormal returns) quantifies the impact of the stadium naming rights deal on the share price.

Several of these studies concluded that there can be a short-term increase in share price on the day that a stadium naming rights deal is announced, with deals of a longer duration appearing to have a greater impact (Clark et al., 2002; Goldberg et al., 2019). However, the impact on share price appears rather short-lived and studies examining the extended outlook found that any initial price boost quickly recedes (Becker-Olsen, 2003; Leeds et al., 2007). This suggests that while the signing of a sizeable and high-profile naming rights deal might signal confidence in the company's future by management (Clark et al., 2002), if the main motivation is to increase the long-term return to shareholders or company value, then naming rights sponsorship is no better than any other form of marketing investment (Becker-Olsen, 2003). This does not negate the significant marketing benefits discussed above, but instead highlights that stadium naming rights sponsorship, as with any marketing-related spend, should only be undertaken where it is best suited to achieving the objectives that the sponsor brand desires.

Benefits to rights holders

As with all sponsorship deals, naming rights represent a partnership, in this case, between the naming rights sponsor and the rights holder (the stadium owner). As such, stadia naming rights sponsorship will be even more effective and fruitful as a business relationship if there are benefits to all parties in the transaction. Clearly, rights holders benefit from the significant financial inflows associated with high-value naming rights deals. Furthermore, the long-term nature of many naming rights arrangements gives security to these financial inflows over many years. Many new stadia are also funded, at least in part, through revenue secured from naming rights, meaning that this form of sponsorship can pave the way for sports clubs, organisations, and communities to benefit from the development of new, state-of-the-art facilities. However, there can also be benefits to rights holders that move beyond the direct inflow of cash. This is an aspect of stadia naming rights that is arguably not as well developed or understood as it could be, and many rights holders may be unaware of these other potential benefits when selecting naming rights partners (assuming they have a choice in such matters).

One example of a stadium naming rights deal which brought additional mutual benefits to both the sponsor and the rights holder is that between the Wanda Group and Spanish football club Athletico Madrid. Prior to signing the naming rights deal for the Estadio Wanda Metropolitano, the Wanda Group already had a stake in Athletico Madrid. Here, the naming rights sponsorship was being used as a means of strengthening the existing collaboration between the club and the sponsor. The deal allowed Wanda Group to achieve a range of brand-building objectives, including awareness and image benefits.

Partnering with such a large international brand allowed Athletico Madrid to reinforce its position on the global stage, opening the club up to the profitable Chinese market through Wanda's existing distribution networks and dominance there. It also allowed the club to raise its profile in other international markets where the Wanda Group was present.

Despite these potential benefits, there are some significant differences between sports and geographic markets in terms of the adoption of stadia naming rights deals, as discussed in Chapter 1. Research by the consultancy firm Duff & Phelps (2019) suggests that while 80% of NFL stadia in the USA have naming rights deals, this figure is only 27% in the top-five football leagues in Europe. They conclude that stadia naming rights are underexploited as a potential revenue source, which might suggest a lack of appreciation on the part of rights holders of their value. However, to take a purely financial perspective on this would ignore the range of non-financial considerations that sports teams and organisations have in deciding whether to sell the naming rights to their stadia. As will be discussed in more detail in Chapter 4, the reactions of fans to stadia naming rights differ markedly between newly built and long-established stadia. In terms of the latter, sports teams that play in such longstanding venues must consider the equity that their stadium name possesses and offset this against any potential financial gains from selling the naming rights. For example, English Premier League club Manchester United has repeatedly said that it will not sell the naming rights to its iconic Old Trafford stadium because fans have a very strong attachment to the stadium and its name. In fact, the Old Trafford name is synonymous worldwide with Manchester United and as such has considerable value to the club as a branding device. Any naming rights deal would therefore risk significant backlash from fans as well as close off the use of the historic stadium name as part of the club's marketing activities. The examples discussed above indicate the interdependencies and potential for mutual benefit in naming rights relationships, but also highlight a range of factors that will need to be considered by both sponsor brands and rights holders in any decisions about the sale of stadia naming rights.

Benefits to fans and the local community

Beyond naming rights sponsors and rights holders, naming rights deals can also benefit a wider group of stakeholders including fans and local residents. Signing an eight-year naming rights deal with Docklands Stadium in Melbourne (renamed to Marvel Stadium) allowed Marvel and the seven teams who use the stadium to work together to enhance the fan experience (The Stadium Business, 2019). This involved the creation of a series of Marvel-character-themed installations, such as a Spiderman climbing wall. This deal is a real example of the win-win-win approach to sponsorship advocated by Kim Skildum-Reid (2021). The fans benefit from an improved stadium environment and experience, the sponsor brand benefits from the ability to engage with their target markets in a meaningful way, and the resident teams can use the installations as part of their commitment to enhancing the fan offering.

Thinking more widely, the investment in a new stadium funded through a naming rights deal can bring benefits to the local community where that stadium is located. For example, students and local residents benefited from renovated facilities as a result of the $60 million deal to rename the University of Illinois's Assembly Hall the State Farm Center. On an even larger scale, the investment by Etihad in the area surrounding Manchester City's Etihad Stadium in North West England has been the catalyst for significant urban regeneration, including building many world-class facilities that can be used by the local community. The relationship between Etihad and Manchester City extends beyond merely naming rights, with the airline and the club both owned by Abu-Dhabi's ruling Al-Nahyan family. However, investment into the Etihad Campus (the wider complex of sports and community facilities around Manchester City's Etihad Stadium) demonstrates the potential for naming rights deals to provide a significant cash injection into urban economies, which can support sports teams' efforts to engage with their wider communities.

Conclusion

This chapter has explored the range of objectives that sponsors can pursue through stadia naming rights deals. Using the buying funnel model as a guide, the objectives of brand awareness, brand consideration, sales, and brand loyalty can all, to a greater or lesser extent, be pursued (and achieved) through careful and well-chosen use of stadia naming rights sponsorship. Furthermore, stadia naming rights can help sponsor brands to demonstrate their CSR, although the extent to which this is possible will depend on the nature of the brand involved and their choice of which stadium to sponsor.

The chapter has also discussed how stadia naming rights sponsorship can benefit other parties in the sponsorship relationship, including rights holders, fans, and the wider community – a recognised win-win-win-win situation. As with all forms of sponsorship, the extent to which stadium naming rights sponsorship is successful will depend on a wide range of internal and external factors. Important among these is the activation of the sponsorship, which moves beyond merely putting a brand name on a stadium. The next chapter discusses the role and importance of activation in naming rights sponsorship.

References

Becker-Olsen, K. (2003). Questioning the name game: An event study analysis of stadium naming rights sponsorship announcements. *International Journal of Sports Marketing and Sponsorship, 5*(3), 9–20. https://doi.org/10.1108/IJSMS-05-03-2003-B002

Businesswire. (2021, March 28). Swedbank Arena becomes Friends Arena. https://www.businesswire.com/news/home/20120328005599/en/Swedbank-Arena-becomes-Friends-Arena

Carroll, A. B. (1979). A three-dimensional conceptual model of corporate performance. *Academy of Management Review, 4*(4), 497–505. https://doi.org/10.5465/amr.1979.4498296

Clark, J. M., Cornwell, T. B., & Pruitt, S. W. (2002). Corporate stadium sponsorships, signalling theory, agency conflicts and shareholder wealth. *Journal of Advertising Research, 42*(6), 16–32. https://doi.org/10.2501/JAR.42.6.16

Chen, K. K., & Zhang, J. J. (2012). To name it or not name it: Consumer perspectives on facility naming rights sponsorship in collegiate athletics. *Journal of Issues in Intercollegiate Athletics, 5*, 119–148.

Donlan, L. (2014). An empirical assessment of factors affecting the brand-building effectiveness of sponsorship. *Sport, Business and Management: An International Journal, 4*(1), 6–25. https://doi.org/10.1108/SBM-09-2011-0075

Donlan, L. (2013). The role of brand knowledge in determining sponsorship effectiveness. *Journal of Promotion Management, 19*(2), 241–264. https://doi.org/10.1080/10496491.2013.769474

Duff & Phelps (2019). *Are Football Stadium Naming Rights Undervalued?* https://www.duffandphelps.com/insights/publications/valuation/european-stadium-naming-rights-report-2019

Eddy, T. (2014). Measuring effects of naming-rights sponsorships on college football fans' purchasing intentions. *Sport Management Review, 17*(3), 362–375. https://doi.org/10.1016/j.smr.2013.08.001

Gillooly, L., Medway, D., Warnaby, G. & Roper, S. (2021). 'To us it's still Boundary Park': Fan discourses on the corporate (re)naming of football stadia. *Social & Cultural Geography.* Advance online publication. https://doi.org/10.1080/14649365.2021.1910990

Goldberg, D. M., Deane, J. K., Rakes, T. R., & Rees, L. P. (2019). Marketing investments in sport venue naming rights and the market value of the firm. *International Journal of Sport Management and Marketing, 19*(3–4), 233–252. https://doi.org/10.1504/IJSMM.2019.099785

Gwinner, K. (1997). A model of image creation and image transfer in event sponsorship. *International Marketing Review, 14*(3), 145–158. https://doi.org/10.1108/02651339710170221

Haan, P., & Shank, M. (2004). Consumers' perceptions of NFL stadium naming rights. *International Journal of Sports Marketing and Sponsorship, 5*(4), 25–37. https://doi.org/10.1108/IJSMS-05-04-2004-B004

IEG (2017). *What sponsors want and where dollars will go in 2018.* http://www.sponsorship.com/IEG/files/f3/f3cfac41-2983-49be-8df6-3546345e27de.pdf

Kotler, P., Rackham, N., & Krishnaswamy, S. (2006). Ending the war between sales and marketing. *Harvard Business Review, 84*(7/8), 68–78.

Lardinoit, T., & Derbaix, C. (2001). Sponsorship and recall of sponsors. *Psychology & Marketing, 18*(2), 167–190. https://doi.org/10.1002/1520-6793(200102)18:2<167::AID-MAR1004>3.0.CO;2-I

Leeds, E. M., Leeds, M. A., & Pistolet, I. (2007). A stadium by any other name: The value of naming rights. *Journal of Sports Economics, 8*(6), 581–595. https://doi.org/10.1177/1527002506296546

Light, D., & Young, C. (2014). Habit, memory, and the persistence of socialist-era street names in Postsocialist Bucharest, Romania. *Annals of the Association of American Geographers, 104*(3), 668–685. https://doi.org/10.1080/00045608.2014.892377

Mazodier, M., & Merunka, D. (2012). Achieving brand loyalty through sponsorship: The role of fit and self-congruity. *Journal of the Academy of Marketing Science, 40*(6), 807–820. https://doi.org/10.1007/s11747-011-0285-y

Meyn, T. (2014, January 31). *Tradie superannuation fund Cbus Super spends up big on naming rights for stadium as Skilled signage is removed.* Gold Coast Bulletin. https://www.goldcoastbulletin.com.au/news/gold-coast/tradie-superannuation-fund-cbus-super-spends-up-big-on-naming-rights-for-stadium-as-skilled-signage-is-removed/news-story/7a39c5e3f58d549d01ee75b7ade202bf

Pham, M. T., & Johar, G. V. (2001). Market prominence biases in sponsor identification: Processes and consequentiality. *Psychology & Marketing, 18*(2), 123–143. https://doi.org/10.1002/1520-6793(200102)18:2<123::AID-MAR1002>3.0.CO;2-3

Reysen, S., Snider, J. S., & Branscombe, N. R. (2012). Corporate renaming of stadiums, team identification, and threat to distinctiveness. *Journal of Sport Management, 26*(4), 350–357. https://doi.org/10.1123/jsm.26.4.350

Sirgy, M. J., Lee, D. J., Johar, J. Y., & Tidwell, J. (2008). Effect of self-congruity with sponsorship on brand loyalty. *Journal of Business Research, 61*(10), 1091–1097. https://doi.org/10.1016/j.jbusres.2007.09.022

Skildum-Reid, K. (2021). *Last Generation Sponsorship Redux.* https://powersponsorshipdownloads.com/wp-content/uploads/2020/09/LastGenerationSponsorship.pdf

Smith, G. (2004). Brand image transfer through sponsorship: A consumer learning perspective. *Journal of Marketing Management, 20*(3/4), 457–474. https://doi.org/10.1362/026725704323080498

The Stadium Business. (2019, July 11). *Marvel Stadium's 'Step-Change' in Fan Experience.* https://www.thestadiumbusiness.com/2019/07/11/marvel-stadiums-step-change-fan-experience/

Tsordia, C., Papadimitriou, D., & Parganas, P. (2018). The influence of sport sponsorship on brand equity and purchase behavior. *Journal of Strategic Marketing, 26*(1), 85–105. https://doi.org/10.1080/0965254X.2017.1374299

Woisetschläger, D. M., Backhaus, C., & Cornwell, T. B. (2017). Inferring corporate motives: How deal characteristics shape sponsorship perceptions. *Journal of Marketing, 81*(5), 121–141. https://doi.org/10.1509/jm.16.0082

3 Activating Naming Rights Sponsorships

What is activation?

There are a number of definitions for sponsorship activation. Activation (or leveraging/servicing) has been referred to as any additional investment in a sponsorship beyond the rights fee for activities that communicate the relationship (O'Reilly & Lafrance Horning, 2013). Previously, the element of investment had been overlooked by Cornwell et al. (2005, p. 36), who defined activation as 'collateral communication of a brand's relationship with a property'. These definitions are typical of those that tend to drive academic work on activation, but we note again that some individuals, particularly some industry professionals, reserve the term 'activation' for more highly interactive marketing activities (e.g., product sampling, hospitality, complementary events). As such, these people do not consider, say, static signage or branding shown on video boards to be activations, whereas these would typically be considered activations using the academic definitions. Here, we will follow the more inclusive/exhaustive definitions that tend to be more widely accepted when considering both academic and industry audiences.

Regardless of how exactly activation is defined in terms of qualifying activities, there is widespread agreement between both academics and industry practitioners that activation is key to generating positive impact from sponsorships (Kim et al., 2015). The more sponsors spend on activation, the more likely the sponsorship is to be successful (O'Reilly & Lafrance Horning, 2013). Although spending is required, it alone is not sufficient to guarantee success, as content and communication are key activation campaign factors (Dreisbach et al., 2021). Common activation communication channels include social media, public relations, hospitality, on-site/experiential activities and events, internal communications, digital/mobile promotions, traditional

DOI: 10.4324/9781003111849-3

advertising, business-to-business (B2B) activities, sales promotion offers, and direct marketing (Dees et al., 2021).

Historically, many early naming rights deals were very narrowly implemented to include mainly just the name of the stadium and associated signage. As such, early naming sponsors were largely missing out on opportunities to achieve other objectives beyond broad awareness. Although such deals with minimal 'extra' activation still exist, the majority of deals now feature the stadium name as the most broadly visible piece of a more comprehensive partnership. Philips Arena in Atlanta, Georgia, USA, a landmark deal in 1999 that cost approximately $9 million per year, was one of the first naming rights deals to be part of a broader integrated marketing strategy. In addition to having the name, Philips provided all electronic equipment for the arena (e.g., the scoreboard), and also had a retail/showcase area on the concourse to feature new product offerings, allowing fans to experience them first-hand. Similarly, as part of their 2003 naming rights deal for the new arena in Houston, Texas, USA, Toyota was able to convert luxury suites into a showroom featuring cars that were open to the arena bowl and visible by spectators in their seats, as well as another showroom space on the concourse where fans could get up close to the vehicles.

The Philips and Toyota deals became exemplars for integrating a naming sponsor's products into a facility, a strategy that has since been copied numerous times across the world. This activation type is particularly popular with automobile brands, which still use the Toyota deal as a template. Philips, on the other hand, acts as both an example of innovation but also a cautionary tale. Given that it was important for the featured products to remain current, it became expensive and laborious to switch out the many integrated products that Philips had within the arena. This is in contrast to Toyota having to only move around a couple of cars each year. Thus, the lessons learned from these early deals are still relevant today.

Throughout the rest of this chapter we will outline some theories that explain how activations can help brands, and cover the types of activation that naming rights sponsors are using to make their deals more successful. Specific examples of notable partnerships will be integrated throughout.

Why does activation work?

The effectiveness of activation can be explained by a number of different theories from marketing, social psychology, and other related fields. These theories are obviously relevant to academics and researchers, but it is important for practitioners to be aware of them as well. By understanding how individuals process information and experiences, industry professionals can better tailor activation strategies that will benefit brands. To bring back a theory from Chapter 2, activation plays a key role in brand image transfer by creating additional brand associations for the sponsor. For example, Levi's created a 49ers collection of products alongside their naming rights agreement for Levi's Stadium, home of the San Francisco 49ers, and had everyone from the stadium employees to the team mascot dressed in Levi's clothing. By integrating their products with important team brand associations, they were attempting to facilitate positive image transfer from the team's brand to their own. We will provide an overview of a few more relevant theories here and connect them to activation. It should be noted that several of these theories sound similar on the surface, but there are subtle differences between them.

The 'mere exposure effect'

The mere exposure effect says that individuals' recall of a stimulus is improved simply through repeated exposure, which can also lead to more favourable attitudes towards the stimulus itself (Wakefield et al., 2007). This includes incidental exposure of which a person is not consciously aware – thus, when fans are paying attention to a game, the mere exposure effect suggests that by hearing the name of the stadium mentioned or seeing signage in passing, awareness and liking are still being improved. Consequently, the more activation strategies that a naming sponsor engages in, the more mere exposure can work in the background to improve brand outcomes.

Stadium names also receive frequent mentions in media, are seen on maps and road signs, and are visible from highways. Thus, even non-sports fans, who drive by a given stadium, are exposed to the sponsor through their proximity to these important landmarks and their signage. By communicating the name through various media, as well as other activation strategies that will reach more than just fans of the teams that play in the stadium, mere exposure suggests that these broader groups of people will become 'used to' the name, and consequently more aware, and in favour, of the brand.

Evaluative conditioning

Evaluative conditioning refers to how people's perception of a stimulus can change when it is paired with another (positive or negative) stimulus. Thus, when a parent brand that is viewed positively (e.g., a sports organisation or team) is connected to a secondary brand (e.g., a sponsor), evaluative conditioning suggests that those positive feelings will subconsciously transfer to the secondary brand (Tsiotsou et al., 2014). This is particularly true when consumers are highly attached to the parent brand, which is an obvious strength of sports brands.

In addition to the partnership itself, activation can also lead to increased goodwill for a brand via evaluative conditioning. When sponsors are involved with activations that have symbolic or social benefits for fans of the team, it makes the sponsorship seem more altruistic; and fans, therefore, perceive the partnership more positively (Dreisbach et al., 2021). An emerging trend that appears intended to capitalise on this effect is placing alternative names on stadia, rather than using the sponsor's brand name. Examples, which were discussed in the context of CSR objectives in Chapter 2, include the Friends Arena in Solna, Sweden (sponsored by Swedbank, but donated to the Friends Foundation, a charitable organisation to which Swedbank is a major benefactor) and the Climate Pledge Arena (sponsored by Amazon, but used to highlight Amazon's efforts to fight global climate change).

Social identity theory

Social identity theory proposes that the formal and informal social groups to which people belong (or perceive themselves as belonging to) are important aspects of their self-concept, and have substantial impacts on self-esteem (Lock & Heere, 2017). This theory is often used to explain the concept of team identification, which refers to the emotional connection that fans have with sports organisations. As such, fans that become highly identified with a team see themselves as an extension of the team, and are positively biased towards other fans of the team (termed the in-group), but are also negatively biased towards non-fans of the team (termed the out-group – e.g., fans of rival teams).

If a naming rights sponsor can position itself in a way that it appears to be supporting the team, then it is possible for fans to begin to perceive the sponsor as a member of the in-group. In addition to holding the name to the stadium, well-rounded activation strategies that allow the brand to connect itself with the team in more meaningful, symbolic ways may signal to fans that the sponsor identifies with the team. If so, fans will have more positive attitudes towards the sponsor. Conversely, if brands purchase the name to the stadium and do little else to activate the sponsorship, this could be seen by fans as an inauthentic partnership, or strictly selfish commercial intent. Thus, highly identified fans may not accept this sponsor as part of the in-group. Although the brand would still be able to capitalise on some of the brand awareness impacts mentioned previously (e.g., via mere exposure), it is unlikely that positive affective transfer would occur.

Examples of activation types

As mentioned previously, early naming rights deals were usually limited to the facility name, with the brand also receiving some added benefits like tickets (often to suites) and/or access to hospitality areas as part of the deal. Although these value-added pieces are still commonplace, naming sponsors have become much more involved in activation. There is clearly a long and varied menu of activation strategies available to naming sponsors, so it is worth highlighting that the sponsor's objectives should always be the key factor driving the adoption of an activation strategy. Further, the best activation strategies tend to adopt a multifaceted approach, whereby different types of activations are integrated into a holistic campaign. Not only does such an approach offer more diversified ways to connect with relevant targets, but it can also assist with satisfying multiple sponsor objectives.

In this section, we will offer some notable examples of activations that naming sponsors have employed, grouped by broad activation types. Although most naming rights sponsors are primarily B2C companies, we will highlight a few cases of activations that have a B2B focus as well. As alluded to previously, many of the brands that are implementing 'best practice' activation strategies contain elements that fit within different categories of our typology, and/or single activations that can fit within multiple categories. In the latter case, we have attempted to classify these by their most dominant characteristic.

Premium asset bundling

In most cases, naming sponsors will secure rights to have other signage inside a facility, in addition to exterior signage showcasing the building name. Some naming sponsors have taken this one step further to secure other premium assets from the sports organisation. For example, a number of naming sponsors have also purchased shirt sponsorship, with Emirates Airlines being one of the first to do so back in 2006 with Arsenal F.C. This relationship has become one of the longest stadium/shirt deals in professional sport, and has been found to be the most recognisable and best fitting shirt sponsorship in the Premier League (Carp, 2019). It seems reasonable to suggest that Emirates holding both pieces of premium inventory, in addition to the length of the deal, were likely contributors to these findings. Similarly, although Jeep is the main shirt sponsor for Juventus Football Club, Allianz (the club's stadium sponsor) secured rights to sponsor the team's training and warmup shirts. While not as visible as the main shirt sponsor, training/warmup kits are still premium pieces of inventory that generate significant exposure for the sponsor during the team's games.

Other premium inventory targeted by naming rights sponsors includes hospitality spaces and club areas. These assets are of particular value for companies that have B2B-related objectives. For example, at the new Q2 Stadium in Austin, Texas, USA, Q2 (a primarily B2B financial services and holding company) also secured the name to the Q2 Field club, which is a premium hospitality space located near the players' benches and locker rooms.

Sponsor product integration

In order to generate new business, and also to reward existing customers, some naming sponsors have offered additional benefits to those who use their products and/or belong to their loyalty programmes. For example, Bankwest Mastercard holders received money off food and beverages when they used their cards for purchases at the then Bankwest Stadium in Sydney, Australia.[1] Bankwest cardholders were also offered exclusive promotions and giveaways for tickets to events at the stadium. Although a great number of banks and credit card companies activate their sponsorships in similar ways, this is one of the few examples where such a strategy included naming rights integration. Loyalty programmes are similarly critical for hotels, but hotel brands are less common purchasers of naming rights. One example is Accor Arena in Paris, France, where AccorHotels club members receive a number of exclusive benefits, content and services, including ticket pre-sale access (Accor, 2022).

Going one step further, Marvel Stadium has the Marvel Vault, Australia's only Marvel retail store, which is open on both event and non-event days. This retail space brings the sponsor's products right into the stadium, generating more foot traffic for both itself as well as the stadium. Beyond this, the Marvel Vault, as well as Marvel's naming sponsorship more generally, provides a powerful example of another type of activation – integration of the sponsor into the fan experience. It is to these types of activations that we will turn in the next two sections.

Stadium experience enhancements

Another activation approach taken by naming sponsors is to further integrate themselves into the game-day experience at the facility, beyond simply holding the name to the venue. One way of achieving this is by offering ancillary entertainment options for event attendees. In addition to the retail store mentioned previously, Marvel Stadium has a series of Marvel-branded mini-attractions that serve as entertainment experiences, such as the Spider-Man climbing wall and Marvel Gamerverse (an interactive video game area featuring Marvel-branded arcade games). These attractions are clearly targeted towards enhancing the game-day experience for families and children, particularly those who might be more casual fans of the teams/sports. They also have potential to develop new business for both the brand and stadium tenants. Such offerings provide Marvel exposure to sports fans who may not be as familiar with their products, or conversely they may draw Marvel fans to events that they may not normally attend.

Beyond ancillary entertainment, sponsors have also sought to integrate themselves into the event to enhance the experience of watching the game itself. One example is at the Orange Velodrome in Marseille, France. Orange, a telecommunications provider, placed a 5G antenna in the stadium (as well as additional Wi-Fi terminals) to enhance wireless connectivity for fans (The Stadium Business, 2019). They further leveraged the resultant increase in download speeds to create new 360-degree video streams and virtual reality content, along with enhanced sound experiences (e.g., fans could boost the sound of the ball being kicked in their headphones). In doing so, fans are able to have a new and unique immersive viewing experience, thanks to these new technologies.

While Orange decided to leverage technology to improve the viewing aspect of attending an event, Optus, another telecommunications brand, decided to focus more on the non-viewing aspects of attending an event at Optus Stadium in Perth, Australia. Similarly to Orange, Optus also placed a 5G antenna at the stadium, but the functions within their app were focused on logistics, accessibility, and ticketing. With the Optus Stadium app, fans can access their paperless tickets, explore food and beverage menus (with stadium maps for wayfinding), use a real-time public transportation planner, book a tour of the stadium, or win prizes and seat upgrades (Optus Stadium, 2022). As such, the app provides support and information for almost everything fans could need after they leave home on an event day at the stadium.

Fan engagement

As well as augmenting the stadium experience, naming sponsors have turned to technology to engage with fans even more broadly. One of the first examples of a naming rights sponsor focusing primarily on

fan/customer engagement was the award-winning partnership between O2 and the O2 Arena in London, UK. As with the other telecommunications brands mentioned previously, O2 created an app for
customers to choose their own benefits or take advantage of various
activations and promotions. In particular, O2 customers are able to
access advance tickets and priority admission. In addition, there are
on-site benefits such as a private lounge space, and the ability to order food/drink through the app. Consequently, O2 was one of the first
naming sponsors to offer these types of benefits to encourage brand
engagement by customers, through a vehicle that also provides robust
performance metrics back to the brand (Dumais, 2016).

The idea of leveraging a naming rights sponsorship for fan engagement has arguably been taken to the next level at the SAP Arena, a
multi-purpose playing venue for ice hockey and handball clubs in
Mannheim, Germany. SAP is the largest non-American software
company in the world, providing businesses with integrative software
to manage all their operations through one platform. The company
brought this expertise inside the SAP Arena in a variety of ways, including integrating its fan app and point of sale system so that the two
would work together. As such, it was able to integrate systems that
historically have operated separately (e.g., ticketing, concessions, merchandise) to better understand fans' overall behaviour. This allowed
for the development of a more holistic loyalty programme than most
apps can offer, where fans earn points for any purchases they make
at the arena (tickets, merchandise, etc.) that can be subsequently re-
deemed for various rewards. By also implementing proximity marketing, SAP was able to grow fan engagement due to the amount of data
and touchpoints it had for each consumer. In addition, the company
implemented other technologies to track queues for concessions and
restrooms in real time, which fans could view on their devices from
their seats (Bassam, 2018). The SAP sponsorship serves as a prime example of what technology (specifically software) companies can bring
to the event experience through a long-term relationship with a facility, and is a glimpse into what is possible in the future if more of these
kinds of organisations enter the (naming) sponsorship space.

Corporate social responsibility

Following recent trends in sponsorship more generally to follow societal expectations around corporate social responsibility, naming
rights sponsors are beginning to integrate more charitable and/or
community-focused components. Regarding the former, one of the

most notable examples of donating a stadium name to a charity occurred in 2019. Queens Park Rangers Football Club (QPR) in London, UK gifted their naming rights to the Kiyan Prince Foundation, which was selected via online fan nominations and a vote. Kiyan Prince was a QPR youth player who was killed at the age of 15 while breaking up a fight outside his school, and the foundation was set up in his memory to address issues with youth violence (Sky Sports, 2019). Clearly, this cause holds a deep meaning for QPR and its fans, and thus exemplifies a very high fit as a stadium name. In early 2020, FC Barcelona also announced a plan to cede naming rights for its iconic Camp Nou stadium to the club's charitable foundation, with the intention of donating all proceeds to the continued fight against Covid-19 (Lowe, 2020). However, as of the time of writing, no naming partner has been secured, and the club has also disclosed that it is in significant financial trouble, so it is unclear whether the naming rights deal is still a priority.

For-profit organisations are also beginning to integrate charitable initiatives into naming rights sponsorships. FTX, a cryptocurrency exchange that holds naming rights to the FTX Arena in Miami, Florida, USA, recently secured rights for the American football field at the University of California, Berkeley, to be called FTX Field at California Memorial Stadium. In addition to the $17.5 million that FTX paid for the ten-year agreement, which is being paid entirely in cryptocurrency, FTX has also committed funds for various charitable initiatives as part of the deal, including addressing homelessness in Berkeley, which align with the firm's core values (Lee, 2021). In a similar vein, Q2 in Austin, Texas, mentioned previously as the naming partner for Q2 Stadium, home to Austin FC, is allowing fans to vote on where the company should donate $150,000 to non-profit organisations (McCormick, 2021).

Several brands are using their naming rights sponsorships for community development independent of charitable partnerships. In addition to the fan vote on donations mentioned previously, Q2 is also sponsoring a competition to start/accelerate a business plan of a local company as a way to further give back to the community (McCormick, 2021). Although Q2 is primarily a financial services holding and technology company that is largely B2B focused, it supports many community-based initiatives to support underserved populations, including minorities, veterans, and the elderly. Another example of giving back to the community, on an arguably more global scale, is Amazon's deal with the Climate Pledge Arena in Seattle, Washington, USA. In addition to the 'Pledge' in the name, referencing Amazon's stated commitment to reduce its own carbon emissions, the stadium is aiming to produce zero waste, will be powered entirely by renewable electricity, and will work towards achieving a zero-carbon footprint (Climate Pledge Arena, 2022). This deal is a clear example of aligning and communicating corporate values shared by the arena, its tenants, and a naming rights sponsor.

Social media

Social media has become the most frequently used channel for sponsorship activation by brands (Dees et al., 2021). It could be argued that social media is merely a vehicle for the other activation types mentioned in this chapter (e.g., fan engagement). However, given the current prominence of social media in the sponsorship landscape, we feel obliged to offer a few thoughts on its use in activation by naming rights sponsors.

One benefit that naming sponsors enjoy over other sponsoring brands is that stadia names can be woven into many forms of social media posting (e.g., game updates, traffic information), which generates mere exposure for the brand concerned without communicating obvious commercial intent. When other sponsors activate on social media through team accounts (e.g., logos or brand names added to posts, or product promotions), their posts run the risk of being intrusive to users' social media experience, and risk being targeted as advertising by followers. Naming sponsors are more able to sidestep this negative attention due to their connection to the stadium facility and team(s) that play there.

Recent academic research in this area supports the use of team-based accounts to communicate naming rights sponsorships. Of the activation categories examined by Eddy et al. (2021), they found that naming rights-focused tweets from team accounts received the most engagement (via likes and retweets) among six activation types (namely CSR/cause marketing, team-focused sales promotions, brand-focused sales promotions, branded features, passive signage, and naming rights). Thus, naming rights sponsors were receiving more indirect exposure, thanks to message diffusion, than other types of sponsors. As mentioned above, the authors suggested that this increased engagement was due to the fact that naming sponsors could appear in posts that were not focused on advertising since they were highly integrated with the core product (either the team or game-day experience), which is primarily why fans are following team accounts in the first place.

Some facilities also choose to create their own social media presences. One of the most recent examples is the new SoFi Stadium in

Los Angeles, California, USA, which has its own Twitter and Instagram accounts. The Twitter account posts various types of content, including information about upcoming events (e.g., ticket opportunities, parking information), sharing posts from its tenants' accounts, and other content relevant to the local community (e.g., Hispanic Heritage month). Although these accounts offer another touchpoint for the brand to engage with fans through its naming sponsorship, it is unclear whether these stadium-owned accounts are that effective. As of the time of writing, SoFi Stadium had approximately 53,000 Twitter followers, which pales in comparison to its primary tenants, the LA Rams and LA Chargers, which each have approximately 1 million followers. Thus, while a stadium account is likely to be useful, it would appear that any naming rights sponsoring brand enjoys greater impact from indirect posts and mentions (e.g., via team accounts) than from its own content.

Conclusion

This chapter has discussed just a few of the more prominent examples of naming rights sponsors who are doing innovative and effective things with respect to activating their sponsorships. A clear theme for most of these exemplars is that the brands doing the best job are activating in ways that are congruent with their core business and/or values, thereby leveraging what they already do well in new ways. Clearly, we believe telecommunications companies are leading the way with naming rights activation, in large part due to how they can integrate their existing technologies to engage with customers and/or enhance the game-day experience, at a relatively lower cost than brands from other industries. O2, for example, is able to implement its activation strategies for less than it paid for the rights fees (Dumais, 2016), which is contrary to conventional wisdom in sponsorship circles that brands need to be paying at least as much to activate as they do for the rights fee, if not many times more (O'Reilly & Lafrance Horning, 2013). Further, O2 (as well as other telecommunications brands) has been especially active in naming rights sponsorship and activation due to the very competitive nature of its industry, where there is minimal brand differentiation at the product level (i.e., most carriers sell essentially the same line-ups of smartphones). Thus, O2 is able to focus on developing brand loyalty through its activation strategies, rather than continuing to attempt to poach customers from other carriers (which has been standard marketing strategy among telecommunications companies since the industry reached maturity). In summary, we hope that the strategies presented in this chapter will show brands that creative activation of naming rights sponsorships can return significant value with regard to a wide range of objectives.

Note

1 In September 2021, Commonwealth Bank bought the naming rights and the stadium was renamed CommBank Stadium.

References

Accor. (2022). *Entertainment with Added Sparkle!* https://all.accor.com/gb/loyalty-program/program/accorhotels-arena.shtml

Bassam, T. (2018, January 30). *SAP Arena: How a Unique Venue Partnership Is Building the Future of Fan Engagement.* SportsPro. https://www.sportspromedia.com/interviews/sap-arena-venue-partnership-future-fan-engagement/

Carp, S. (2019, January 15). *Arsenal's Emirates Shirt Deal Most Recognised among Fans, Says Report.* SportsPro. https://www.sportspromedia.com/news/premier-league-shirt-sponsors-arsenal-emirates-gambling-companies/

Climate Pledge Arena. (2022). *Sustainability.* https://climatepledgearena.com/sustainability/

Cornwell, T. B., Weeks, C. S., & Roy, D. P. (2005). Sponsorship-linked marketing: Opening the black box. *Journal of Advertising, 34*(2), 21–42. https://doi.org/10.1080/00913367.2005.10639194

Dees, W., Walsh, P., McEvoy, C. D., McKelvey, S., Mullin, B. J., Hardy, S., & Sutton, W. A. (2021). *Sport Marketing* (5th ed.). Human Kinetics.

Dreisbach, J., Woisetschläger, D. M., Backhaus, C., & Cornwell, T. B. (2021). The role of fan benefits in shaping responses to sponsorship activation. *Journal of Business Research, 124,* 780–789. https://doi.org/10.1016/j.jbusres.2018.11.041

Dumais, F. (2016, January 20). *Sponsorship Case Study: O2.* Elevent. https://en.elevent.co/blogs/sponsorship/106454535-o2-sponsorships

Eddy, T., Cork, B. C., Lebel, K., & Hickey, E. H. (2021). Examining engagement with sport sponsor activations on Twitter. *International Journal of Sport Communication, 14*(1), 79–108. https://doi.org/10.1123/ijsc.2020-0019

Kim, Y., Lee, H. W., Magnusen, M. J., & Kim, M. (2015). Factors influencing sponsorship effectiveness: A meta-analytic review and research synthesis. *Journal of Sport Management, 29*(4), 408–425. https://doi.org/10.1123/jsm.2014-0056

Lee, I. (2021, August 23). *FTX Is Paying $17.5 Million in Crypto for the Naming Rights to Cal Memorial Stadium for 10 years.* Business Insider. https://markets.businessinsider.com/news/currencies/ftx-cal-memorial-naming-rights-17-million-cryotcurrency-10-years-2021-8

Lock, D., & Heere, B. (2017). Identity crisis: A theoretical analysis of 'team identification' research. *European Sport Management Quarterly, 17*(4), 413–435. https://doi.org/10.1080/16184742.2017.1306872

Lowe, S. (2020, April 21). *Barcelona to Sell Camp Nou Naming Rights and give Proceeds to Charity*. The Guardian. https://www.theguardian.com/football/2020/apr/21/barcelona-to-sell-camp-nou-naming-rights-and-give-proceeds-to-charity

McCormick, B. (2021, January 25). *Fintech Company Q2 Named Austin FC Stadium Sponsor*. Austin Business Journal. https://www.bizjournals.com/austin/news/2021/01/25/q2-austin-fc-stadium-sponsor.html

Optus Stadium. (2022). *The Optus Stadium App*. https://optusstadium.com.au/the-stadium/optus-stadium-app

O'Reilly, N., & Horning, D. L. (2013). Leveraging sponsorship: The activation ratio. *Sport Management Review, 16*(4), 424–437. https://doi.org/10.1016/j.smr.2013.01.001

Sky Sports. (2019, June 7). *QPR to rename Loftus Road as The Kiyan Prince Foundation Stadium*. https://www.skysports.com/football/news/11711/11736735/qpr-to-rename-loftus-road-as-the-kiyan-prince-foundation160stadium

The Stadium Business. (2019, November 8). *Marseille and Orange Target Fan Experience with Velodrome 5G venture*. https://www.thestadiumbusiness.com/2019/11/08/marseille-orange-target-fan-experience-velodrome-5g-venture/

Tsiotsou, R. H., Alexandris, K., & Cornwell, T. B. (2014). Using evaluative conditioning to explain corporate co-branding in the context of sport sponsorship. *International Journal of Advertising, 33*(2), 295–327. https://doi.org/10.2501/IJA-33-2-295-327

Wakefield, K. L., Becker-Olsen, K., & Cornwell, T. B. (2007). I spy a sponsor: The effects of sponsorship level, prominence, relatedness, and cueing on recall accuracy. *Journal of Advertising, 36*(4), 61–74. https://doi.org/10.2753/JOA0091-3367360405

4 Fan Reactions to Naming Rights Sponsorship

Sports fans often build strong bonds with their favourite teams, such that they may come to view the team as an extension of themselves (Belk, 1988). This can lead to fans forging deep, personal relationships with sports clubs and, as a result, often holding strong views on all aspects of the way a particular club is run. The signing of naming rights deals is one area where fans may express such opinions, primarily through their acceptance or resistance towards new naming rights sponsors. The reactions of fans can depend on a number of factors, including the fit between the naming rights sponsor and the club, the age of the stadium, the scale of financial inflows generated by the naming rights deal, and their level of identification with the club. This chapter will explore the different ways that fans might react to the signing of naming rights sponsorship deals, detail factors influencing these reactions, and offer insight into what sponsors and rights holders can do to facilitate greater acceptance.

Consequences of fan acceptance and resistance towards naming rights sponsorship

It is undoubtedly in the best interests of naming rights holders and sponsors for fans to accept a naming rights deal. Fans' acceptance of a (new) corporate name for a stadium leads to a significant positive impact for sponsors, as it means they are more likely to achieve their range of objectives as detailed in Chapter 2. Equally, for the rights holders, a corporate name that is accepted by fans and achieves a sponsor's objectives is more likely to result in a positive and potentially lucrative renewal of the naming rights deal when the time comes. Even if a given naming rights sponsor decides not to renew, a track record of a successful naming rights deal with widespread fan acceptance is likely to attract other potential sponsorship partners.

DOI: 10.4324/9781003111849-4

By contrast, where fans are resistant to a corporate stadium name, this can potentially undermine the success, or even the viability, of a naming rights deal, and may even result in potential harm to the sponsor brand through negative media coverage. Highly identified fans, defined as those having a strong psychological connection to a team (Wann et al., 1999), often view the renaming of a stadium with a corporate name as a threat to their team's distinctiveness (Reysen et al., 2012). This may be particularly the case where a historic stadium is being renamed – something examined later in the chapter – but can occur with any corporate renaming where fans feel a distinctive part of their team's identity is being lost.

Fan resistance can manifest itself in numerous ways. Where fans dislike or disapprove of a corporate stadium name, they can express their anger by refusing to adopt the (new) corporate name or, in more extreme cases, through protests. For example, in 2019, fans of German Bundesliga team Werder Bremen protested in the city centre and outside the club's stadium against its renaming from Weserstadion to Wohninvest Weserstadion. Fan protests also surfaced in 1995 following the renaming of Candlestick Park, home of MLB team the San Francisco Giants, to 3Com Park. There were also protests outside the ground of English Premier League club Newcastle United in 2011, when news broke of a deal to rename the historic St James' Park stadium the Sports Direct Arena. Here, fans displayed their anger by spray painting the original name back onto the stadium's external walls (BBC, 2012). As a footnote to this incident, a year later, Newcastle United signed a major sponsorship deal with payday loan company Wonga – which also covered aspects such as shirt sponsorship – which announced that, as part of the deal the St James' Park name would be reinstated. In some cases, the weight of fan sentiment towards a naming rights sponsor may be considered so problematic that rights holders and/or sponsors decide (or are forced) to terminate a naming rights deal early. This was the case with Florida Atlantic University and its deal with GEO Group, which will be discussed in more detail in the next section on sponsorship fit.

The motives for rights holders to seek out naming rights sponsors for their stadia are largely driven by financial imperatives. However, as discussed in Chapter 2, there are other benefits to rights holders from naming rights deals. Similarly, the benefits to naming rights sponsors can be many if the deal is successful, although the above examples of more negative fan responses to naming rights deals illustrate that success is not guaranteed. As might be expected, there are various factors that can influence fans' reactions to stadia naming rights sponsorships and these will be discussed in detail in the remainder of this chapter.

Factors affecting fans' reactions to stadia naming rights sponsorships

Sponsorship fit

It is not uncommon to hear fans and commentators utter phrases such as 'it's just not the right fit for the club' when discussing a new sponsorship deal. In sponsorship, the concept of fit is crucial – it exerts a significant impact over the effectiveness of naming rights and other sponsorship forms. There are a range of competing synonyms for fit, including congruence, relatedness, match-up, and similarity. Sponsorship fit can be defined as the match between a sponsor and a rights holder (Becker-Olsen & Hill, 2006), or the logic of a particular brand sponsoring a particular property (Olson & Thjømøe, 2011). Therefore, we can think of fit in a naming rights sponsorship context as a situation where it makes sense that a sponsor would partner with their chosen rights holder.

Fit can be divided into multiple types or bases, including functional, image, and geographic fit. For example, when sportswear manufacturer Macron was the naming rights sponsor for English football club Bolton Wanderers, there was functional fit in that it made sense that a sporting brand would sponsor a sports club. Geographic fit was (at least partially) achieved when Scotiabank acquired the naming rights to what became known as Scotiabank Arena (formerly Air Canada Centre), home of the Toronto Raptors (NBA), Toronto Maple Leafs (NHL), and Toronto Rock (National Lacrosse League; NLL). In this case, there is a geographic connection between the stadium and the sponsor brand, which is headquartered in the city of Toronto.

While functional and geographic fit might be more objectively identifiable, image fit relates to a congruence between the brand images or personalities of the sponsor and the rights holder. Therefore, image fit might be deemed more subjective, and ultimately it relates to those cases where someone believes 'it just works for this brand to sponsor that stadium'. The concept of image fit is perhaps best demonstrated by using an example of where it was lacking. Consider the case of Florida Atlantic University. This institution signed a naming rights agreement with GEO Group, which operates a number of prisons across the USA. There was strong geographic fit between the two, with both the university and GEO Group being based in Boca Raton, Florida.

However, the naming rights deal prompted anger relating to public and student accusations of human rights abuses at GEO Group prison facilities (Patterson, 2013). Fans quickly began referring to the stadium as 'Owlcatraz' in online discussions, playing on the team's mascot Owlsley and the famous Alcatraz prison. These reactions suggest that fans did not feel there was a fit between the brand image of the university and that of GEO Group. Eventually, this naming rights deal was withdrawn. The example illustrates not only what is meant by image fit but also how stadia naming rights holders need to ensure they consider all bases of fit when making naming rights sponsorship decisions.

The role of fit in shaping fans' responses to stadia naming rights sponsorship can be understood using congruity theory (Sirgy, 1986). This suggests that people value harmony or consistency in their thoughts and feelings and so are motivated to seek consistency across different pieces of information that they see paired together. In the case of stadia naming rights sponsorship, fans therefore value consistency between the image or associations they hold of the sponsor and of the rights holder. Where that consistency occurs (i.e., where there is a high degree of sponsorship fit), fans are likely to hold more positive attitudes and feelings towards the sponsor and are thus likely to be more accepting of a naming rights deal. By contrast, where fans feel that consistency does not exist, they are likely to be resistant towards the naming rights deal. Research on the role of sponsorship fit in shaping fans' reactions to stadia naming rights sponsorship has suggested they see geographic fit as being particularly important in influencing their attitudes towards any given deal. However, if geographic fit is not present, fans will work to seek out additional bases of fit such as image in order to achieve a state of consistency (Gillooly et al., 2020).

The fit between a naming rights sponsor and a stadium (rights holder) may also be shaped by fans' prior attitudes towards the sponsor brand (Nakazawa et al., 2016) and towards the commercialisation of sport itself (Woisetschläger et al., 2014). Therefore, prior to entering into a naming rights sponsorship deal, both the potential sponsor and the rights holder would be well advised to undertake some research with fans to explore their existing attitudes. A failure to do this might lead to fans resisting the naming rights sponsorship, through means already discussed. Where fans do not hold negative attitudes towards the potential naming rights sponsor, but where fit is not immediately evident, it can be created or emphasised through activation. As discussed in the previous chapter, activation allows naming rights sponsors to articulate their connection and commitment to the club. In so doing, brands can shape fans' perceptions of sponsorship fit, thereby contributing to greater fan acceptance of associated naming rights deals.

As an illustration of the complexity involved in renaming a stadium through a naming rights deal, consider the case of English Football League club Forest Green Rovers. Known widely as being the world's first vegan and carbon neutral professional sports team, in 2020 Forest Green signed a sponsorship deal with smoothie brand Innocent. This included naming rights to the club's stadium, The New Lawn. Seizing the opportunity for fan engagement, Innocent ran a poll on social media to decide on the stadium's new name. A large number of suggestions were received and potentially as a joke, but also indicating a possible wave of anti-corporate sentiment, the suggestion with the most votes through the social media poll was 'Kevin' – an obvious departure from traditional stadia names and the proposed format of the 'Innocent [insert name here] Stadium'. Eventually, a vote among club season ticket holders agreed on the name the 'Innocent New Lawn' (The Stadium Business, 2020). This illustrates the power of fan engagement in the stadium naming process, which in this case generated significant PR for both the club and the Innocent brand. Engaging in activation right from the start of the naming rights deal announcement provides sponsors with an opportunity to shape an on-going campaign and build a dialogue with fans from the outset.

Place-based connections

A second factor which can influence fans' reactions to corporate naming rights sponsorships is their connection to the local area and/or the stadium itself. Research has suggested that when fans feel a strong connection to the local area where the stadium is located, resistance to its corporate renaming may increase (Woisetschläger et al., 2014). A stadium and its surrounding locality are places to which fans may feel a strong attachment (Reysen et al., 2012). In this regard, Boyd (2000) refers to stadia as 'memory places' with the name of a stadium representing that relationship between fans, a club, and the town or city in which it is located. Where fans perceive that renaming a stadium after a corporate brand represents a threat to that relationship, they are likely to resist this new name, perhaps by protesting or through behaviours such as refusing to use it, and/or continuing to call the stadium by its previous (original) name. In the case of Newcastle United's stadium renaming to the Sports Direct Arena, as discussed above, there were many of these place-based connections at play. St James'

Park as a stadium has a long history in the city of Newcastle, being the club's home since 1892. Newcastle is also a city with a very strong identity, of which the football club is a significant part, and, therefore, the stadium is strongly embedded in the culture of the local community. The corporate renaming of St James' Park therefore disrupted fans' place-related and long-engrained patterns of speech and behaviour; and this, in part, explains why the Sports Direct Arena name was never successful. Where brands have gained greater traction in achieving fan acceptance for their stadia naming rights sponsorships is for newly built stadia.

New versus established stadia

As indicated above, when a sports stadium has existed for many years then fans will have formed strong attachments to it as a place – a place for which they may have many fond (and some not so fond) memories. For example, it is not uncommon to hear sports fans talk about famous matches that took place at a stadium or reminisce about the first time they took their child to watch a game there. This helps explain why fans are more resistant to the corporate renaming of long-established stadia through sponsorship than they are towards a corporate name on a newly built venue (Gillooly et al., 2020). For example, contrast the case of the newly built Reebok Stadium,[1] home of Bolton Wanderers, with that of Candlestick Park in San Francisco. Fans of Bolton Wanderers displayed a general acceptance of the corporate name for a stadium where they had no memories. This made it easier for them to embrace the naming rights sponsorship and the financial resources it delivered for their club. We can contrast that with the fan protests mentioned above, which accompanied the decision to rename the historic Candlestick Park to 3Com Park. Candlestick Park, built in 1960 and located on Candlestick Point, had been home to both MLB and NFL teams as well as playing host to a series of major music and cultural events. Consequently, by the time of the naming rights deal in 1995, fans had accumulated a long history of memories and attachment to the stadium. In short, for fans who feel a strong sense of place attachment to a historic stadium, the act of renaming it through sponsorship can represent a threat to their accumulated memories.

   The greater fan acceptance of naming rights sponsorships for newly built stadia is echoed in the willingness of sponsors to enter into naming rights agreements for such venues (DeSchriver & Jensen, 2003). If a corporate sponsor takes over the naming rights of an established stadium with an existing name, then it faces a significant challenge in building awareness of the new name and usurping the previous one in the utterances of fans, media commentators, and local residents. In many cases, the persistence of a previous stadium name in everyday speech is also a matter of habit (Light & Young, 2014) and should not be confused with active resistance. Nevertheless, for naming rights sponsors to reap the benefits of their sponsorship, gaining that name awareness is crucial, as discussed in Chapter 2. For a new stadium, where no prior name exists, building this awareness can be done relatively easily through effective management of media mentions and activation. However, new stadia with no prior name are rare and, in most cases, a naming rights sponsor will take over the rights from a non-corporate name or from another brand. Here, naming rights sponsors face the more difficult challenge of cementing the new name in everyday, popular and media discourse, and it is likely that considerable activation and promotion of the new name will be required to achieve this (as discussed in Chapter 3). The rights holder can also help in this regard, by reinforcing the new name among fans and wider stakeholders and proactively working with the media to ensure the stadium name is represented accurately in all communications.

Scale and level of financial involvement from naming rights sponsor

Another factor which plays an important role in fans' likelihood of accepting stadia naming rights sponsorships is the scale and/or impact of the financial investment being made by the sponsor. If fans perceive that significant benefits will accrue to the club as a result of a naming rights deal, then any resistance is reduced (Woisetschläger et al., 2014). Importantly, this does not simply concern the absolute financial amount of the naming rights sponsorship deal, but rather the relative impact it will have on the club. For example, in the case of the renaming of English football club Oldham Athletic's Boundary Park stadium to SportsDirect.com Park, while not overwhelmingly positive, many fans displayed a degree of reluctant acceptance of the new name based on the impact that the sponsorship revenue would have on the club's ability to survive (i.e., pay the bills) and potentially thrive (i.e., buy new players; Gillooly et al., 2020). Where fans do not see the naming rights sponsorship deal as making a significant enough impact to warrant the trade-off of the stadium name, then their resistance to the deal and towards the naming rights sponsor will increase. One important point to note here is that the research on the impact of financial involvement has largely been conducted in the context of

European football clubs. However, this effect might be muted in sports contexts with salary caps or other structures where, after a certain point, increasing revenue has a negligible impact on the quality of the team itself. When considering entering into naming rights deals, potential sponsors would be well advised to consider the specific context in which a club operates to understand the likelihood of such factors arising.

Beyond the perceived impact of the naming rights sponsor's financial investment, fans' attitudes towards a naming rights deal can also be shaped by a sponsor's prior financial involvement with the club, through mechanisms such as shirt sponsorship or perhaps a stake in club ownership. When a brand has had such a connection with a club previously, and if this is judged acceptable and successful by the club's fans, then a stadium (re)naming rights deal with the same brand is also more likely to gain fan approval. Certainly, broad acceptance of the 'Etihad' stadium name by fans of English Premier League team Manchester City F.C. has been helped by the fact that this naming rights sponsor was also linked to the club's owners (Gillooly et al., 2020).

The reason for a sponsor's prior involvement in a club having a positive impact on fans' attitudes towards a subsequent naming rights deal can be explained using commitment and consistency theory (Cialdini, 2009). This suggests that fans are inclined to maintain a consistent position to one adopted previously when evaluating new information or making new decisions. Therefore, if fans were accepting of a brand's involvement as a sponsor, for example, of the team shirt or simply as a club sponsor, then they are likely to remain consistent in their attitude towards that brand if and when it scales up its investment in the club to become a naming rights partner. Therefore, brands considering entering the stadia naming rights sponsorship arena might be well advised to consider undertaking lower-level sponsorship deals with a club first in order to facilitate acceptance and nurture positive fan sentiment as a precursor to signing a naming rights deal. This may be particularly pertinent for brands that lack obvious bases of fit as they can establish a connection with the club and its fans through a smaller sponsorship investment and then scale it up once they are an accepted partner.

The notion of a trade-off becomes very pertinent as we discuss the range of factors influencing fans' reactions to stadia naming rights sponsorships. All of the examples discussed in this book represent complex cases and it is unlikely that any one single factor was behind the success or failure of a particular naming rights sponsorship. However, what becomes clear is that fans are not naïve to the commercial realities of sport, and while some may be resistant to what they see as over-commercialisation, many recognise the financial imperatives of running professional sports clubs and facilities and understand that naming rights sponsorship is a source of potentially valuable revenue for their favourite club. Therefore, fans will weigh the financial benefits associated with their club's stadium taking a corporate name against the 'cost', which they may experience in terms of a loss of the team's distinctiveness, a threat to their memories, or indeed a threat to their self-identity as a fan.

Team identification

As mentioned earlier in the chapter, a fan's level of identification with the team can shape his or her reaction to the corporate (re)naming of a stadium where that team plays. For highly identified fans, being a fan of a particular team represents a significant part of their self-concept, which is the way a person thinks of or perceives themselves (Rosenberg, 1979). Such fans might exhibit a strong attachment to the club's stadium as the site of many important events in the club's history. Consequently, they often display greater resistance to the corporate naming or renaming of a stadium because they perceive the name change as a threat to their self-identity as a fan. This was exemplified in research with the fanbase of German football team Borussia Dortmund, which found that highly identified fans were more resistant to the renaming of the Westfalenstadion to Signal Iduna Park (Woisetschläger et al., 2014).

Clearly, for the clubs involved, there are significant benefits to having a highly identified fanbase as these will be the club's most ardent and passionate supporters, and perhaps more likely to share positive word of mouth about the team. However, the same fans are also the most likely to reject a new stadium name as a result of a naming rights sponsorship deal. This presents clubs with a challenge of how to engage their loyal fanbase more positively in the renaming of a stadium, and it is here where activation can again play a role. Clubs and stadium owners should look to work with naming rights sponsors from the outset to promote the benefits of the deal to fans, while also being sensitive to their reactions. It is, therefore, advisable for clubs and facilities considering entering into a naming rights agreement to consult with fans in order to secure their input into the decision-making process. This may not be a course of action routinely undertaken by many clubs at present, as they perhaps feel that they are better placed to take commercial decisions in the best interests of the club. However, fans are a valuable and often highly vocal stakeholder group and so involving them can yield benefits, not only in terms of acceptance, but also in exploring innovative and sustainable options for stadia naming rights sponsorships.

Rivalry

As discussed in Chapter 2, the audience for stadia naming rights sponsorships extends beyond those fans of a team that plays at the venue. One of the interesting dynamics involved with sponsorship of sport, as distinct from other forms of marketing communications, is the aspect of rivalry. Consequently, by associating themselves with a particular team, stadia naming rights sponsors potentially run the risk of alienating fans of rival teams, eliciting negative attitudes and even reducing wider purchase intention towards the sponsoring brand (Bee et al., 2021). However, work on US college American football fans suggests that any negative effects on sponsor image and behavioural intentions towards sponsors may be confined to the small number of very highly identified fans of a team's arch-rivals (Eddy et al., 2019). Therefore, we can reasonably surmise that less involved fans are likely to hold minimal animosity towards the naming rights partners of other clubs. In fact, the associated brand exposure benefits in such situations will most likely outweigh any potential harm to that sponsoring brand; if this was not the case then naming rights sponsorship would be a very risky business. That said, potential naming rights sponsors should always consider the rivalries and strength of fan identification associated with particular clubs when considering naming rights deals.

A potential solution for naming rights sponsors keen to overcome any anger towards their brand from rival fans might be to sponsor multiple stadia in order to appeal to a wider fan base. However, while it may seem appealing to attempt to sponsor, for example, the stadia of both rival teams in a particular city, such a strategy could also pose some risks. Evidence from a case whereby telecommunications company NTL sponsored the shirts of both rival Glasgow football teams Rangers and Celtic indicated that while the joint sponsorship brought brand awareness benefits, it did not lead to any benefits in terms of attitudes towards the sponsor (Davies et al., 2006). As already discussed, one of the issues that fans sometimes have with stadia naming rights sponsorship is its threat to the distinctiveness of their team (Reysen et al., 2012). By sponsoring the stadia of two rival teams, a naming rights partner risks threatening this distinctiveness even further and such a plan may end up as a costly endeavour, both in monetary and brand/reputational value terms.

As many sports venues play host to multiple teams, a better solution for brands seeking to reach a wider audience might be to undertake a naming rights deal with a multi-sport stadium. As an example, the Capital One Arena in Washington DC is home to the Washington Capitals NHL team as well as the NBA team the Washington Wizards and the men's basketball team from Georgetown University. While sponsoring multi-sport venues such as this does not address the issue of anger towards the sponsor from rival team fans, it does put the brand in front of a wider range of fan bases, meaning brands can leverage the naming rights benefits across multiple customer segments.

Conclusion

This chapter has explored the different ways that fans may react to the announcement of a stadium naming rights sponsorship deal for the home of their favourite club. These can be spread across a continuum from acceptance through to resistance, with degrees of more reluctant or begrudging acceptance in between. There are ways that clubs as rights holders and potential naming rights sponsors can try to influence fans' perceptions of stadia naming rights sponsorships and these have been explored both in this chapter and in Chapter 3 in the context of activation.

This chapter has also discussed the range of factors which shape fans' reactions to stadia naming rights sponsorships. Drawing on congruity theory, the importance of sponsorship fit in shaping fan reactions was discussed, alongside other factors identified through empirical research across diverse international contexts, including the newness of a stadium, fans' level(s) of identification with the team, place attachment, and the scale and impact of financial investment. Clearly, it is pertinent for clubs and other rights holders to have a comprehensive awareness of these factors, and the inherent complexity that their intersections bring, as well as to have a detailed understanding of the views and preferences of their fans when entering into naming rights agreements. Therefore, the next chapter will explore both the process and criteria involved in selecting a naming rights partner.

Note

1 Subsequently renamed Macron Stadium in 2014 and the University of Bolton Stadium in 2018, as discussed in Chapter 2.

References

BBC. (2012, February 17). *St James' Park graffiti: Michael Atkinson Admits Painting Stadium.* http://www.bbc.co.uk/news/uk-england-tyne-17077966

Becker-Olsen, K. L., & Hill, R. P. (2006). The impact of sponsor fit on brand equity: The case of nonprofit service providers. *Journal of Service Research, 9*(1), 73–83. https://doi.org/10.1177/1094670506289532

Bee, C., King, J., & Stornelli, J. (2021). Are you with us or against us? The role of threat and anger in sport sponsorship. *Journal of Business Research, 124*, 698–707. https://doi.org/10.1016/j.jbusres.2019.02.048

Belk, R. W. (1988). Possessions and the extended self. *Journal of Consumer Research, 15*(2), 139–168. https://doi.org/10.1086/209154

Boyd, J. (2000). Selling home: Corporate stadium names and the destruction of commemoration. *Journal of Applied Communication Research, 28*(4), 330–346. https://doi.org/10.1080/00909880009365580

Cialdini, R. B. (2009). *Influence: Science and Practice* (5th ed.). Pearson Education.

Davies, F., Veloutsou, C., & Costa, A. (2006). Investigating the influence of a joint sponsorship of rival teams on supporter attitudes and brand preferences. *Journal of Marketing Communications, 12*(1), 31–48. https://doi.org/10.1080/13527260500264574

DeSchriver, T. D., & Jensen, P. E. (2003). What's in a name? Price variation in sport facility naming rights. *Eastern Economic Journal, 29*(3), 359–376. https://www.jstor.org/stable/40325421

Eddy, T., Reams, L., & Dwyer, B. (2019). Attitudes toward rival teams' naming-rights sponsors: The influence of perceived strength of rivalry. In C. T. Havard (Ed.), *Understanding Rivalry and Its Influence on Sports Fans* (pp. 182–204). IGI Global.

Gillooly, L., Medway, D., Warnaby, G., & Grimes, A. (2020). The importance of context in understanding football fans' reactions to corporate stadia naming right sponsorships. *European Journal of Marketing, 54*(7), 1501–1522. https://doi.org/10.1108/EJM-03-2018-017

Light, D., & Young, C. (2014). Habit, memory, and the persistence of socialist-era street names in postsocialist Bucharest, Romania. *Annals of the American Association of Geographers, 104*(3), 668–685. https://doi.org/10.1080/00045608.2014.892377

Nakazawa, M., Yoshida, M., & Gordon, B. S. (2016). Antecedents and consequences of sponsor-stadium fit: Empirical evidence from a non-historic stadium context in Japan. *Sport, Business and Management: An International Journal, 6*(4), 407–423. https://doi.org/10.1108/SBM-08-2015-0025

Olson, E. L., & Thjømøe, H. M. (2011). Explaining and articulating the fit construct in sponsorship. *Journal of Advertising, 40*(1), 57–70. https://doi.org/10.2753/JOA0091-3367400104

Patterson, C. (2013, April 2). GEO Group withdraws naming rights gift for FAU Stadium. https://www.cbssports.com/college-football/news/geo-group-withdraws-naming-rights-gift-for-fau-stadium/

Reysen, S., Snider, J. S., & Branscombe, N. R. (2012). Corporate renaming of stadiums, team identification, and threat to distinctiveness. *Journal of Sport Management, 26*(4), 350–357. https://doi.org/10.1123/jsm.26.4.350

Rosenberg, M. (1979). *Conceiving the self.* Basic Books.

Sirgy, M. J. (1986). *Self-congruity: Toward a theory of personality and cybernetics*. Praeger Publishers.

The Stadium Business. (2020, October 19). *Forest Green's home to become the 'Innocent New Lawn'*. https://www.thestadiumbusiness.com/2020/10/19/forest-greens-home-to-become-the-innocent-new-lawn/

Wann, D. L., Fahl, C. L., Erdmann, J. B., & Littleton, J. D. (1999). Relationship between identification with the role of sport fan and trait aggression. *Perceptual and Motor Skills, 88*(3_suppl), 1296–1298. https://doi.org/10.2466/pms.1999.88.3c.1296

Woisetschläger, D. M., Haselhoff, V. J., & Backhaus, C. (2014). Fans' resistance to naming right sponsorships: Why stadium names remain the same for fans. *European Journal of Marketing, 48*(7/8), 1487–1510. https://doi.org/10.1108/EJM-03-2012-0140

5 Selecting a Naming Rights Partner

As we have seen throughout the book so far, the decision to engage in naming rights sponsorship is a significant one, both in terms of financial investment and the potential impact it can have on a brand, both positive and negative. Therefore, neither sponsors nor rights holders should enter into an agreement without a careful appraisal of exactly what the deal will entail, the rights on offer, and the likely risk-reward ratio. Many of the factors feeding into the decision of whether to sign a stadium naming rights deal, and with whom, have been addressed in previous chapters. These include an understanding of the objectives a brand (and a rights holder) wants to pursue, a plan for how the naming rights can be activated, and an appraisal of the fit – all of which can shape fan (and other stakeholder) reactions to a stadium name. This chapter will bring these various considerations together, identifying a series of questions that sponsors and rights holders should ask when considering a stadium naming rights sponsorship deal. These questions highlight the importance of engaging in comprehensive research on the part of both parties prior to signing a naming rights deal. The need for selecting a naming rights partner to be a process informed by research is, therefore, a recurrent theme. Finally, this chapter will examine the emergent body of work on sponsorship renewal, exploring factors which may lead to a greater likelihood of naming rights deals either continuing or ending. Understanding these factors can help practitioners on both sides of the negotiation in their decision-making as to whether (and what) naming rights sponsorship is right for them. While there are likely to be a series of detailed deliberations around exact rights and terms of any deal, it is not our intention here to provide a discussion of the content and intricacies of contract negotiation. Rather, we focus on the more holistic questions that both sponsors and rights holders should ask at the stage of considering a naming rights partnership.

DOI: 10.4324/9781003111849-5

Factors to consider when deciding on a naming rights partner – the sponsor perspective

The first thing that is important to appreciate when brands are considering undertaking a stadium naming rights sponsorship is that any choice will always be constrained by the options available to them. At any one time, there will be some rights holders actively seeking new or replacement naming partners, new stadia will be being built for which naming rights are to be sold, while other stadia will be in the middle of established deals. Therefore, the question of supply and demand becomes pertinent and brands would be well placed to evaluate a suite of potential naming rights opportunities in order to reach a conclusion as to which represents the best available opportunity at that point.

As discussed in Chapter 2, stadia naming rights sponsorship can be used to pursue a range of different objectives. However, the choice of whether to use naming rights sponsorship and, if so, which stadium to sponsor will have a significant impact on both the type of objectives and the extent to which they can be achieved. Stadium naming rights are just one sports property that a brand might choose to sponsor. Sponsorship of other properties such as teams, events, or individual athletes offers an alternative means of achieving a brand's objectives. Similarly, beyond sport, there are numerous sponsorship opportunities in the arts, culture, community, and charity sectors, each of which offer their own unique advantages in terms of achieving objectives and reaching particular target markets. In addition, brands can employ a range of other marketing communications tools such as advertising, social media marketing, public relations, and direct marketing to achieve their objectives. Therefore, it is important for brands to understand which objectives stadium naming rights sponsorship will be effective in meeting, so that an informed decision can be made on whether naming a stadium is the optimal sponsorship vehicle. Therefore, at the earliest stage, brands considering stadium naming rights sponsorship should ask themselves two associated questions:

> *What objectives are our organisation trying to achieve?*
> *Is stadium naming rights sponsorship a suitable vehicle to allow us to achieve these objectives?*

Depending on what a potential naming rights sponsor is looking to achieve, different stadia will likely be more or less suitable depending on their characteristics and what rights are being offered. For example, if a brand is looking for opportunities to increase sales, then they should look for stadia which would include the right to sell the sponsor's products or services on site as part of the naming rights deal. Equally, if a brand was looking to communicate its commitment to the local community and showcase its CSR, then it would be wise to seek out naming rights opportunities at local or grassroots sports facilities. What these examples, and the discussion in Chapter 2, show is that while stadia naming rights sponsorship is flexible as a marketing tool to allow sponsor brands to achieve a range of objectives, it is not a one-size-fits-all marketing solution. The choice of naming rights partner is therefore crucial, and potential sponsors should carefully research the different options available to evaluate which one represents the best opportunity. At this stage in the decision-making process, brands might engage the services of a specialist sponsorship or marketing agency to source and evaluate potential naming rights opportunities. Outsourcing the researching of naming rights opportunities in this way will incur a cost. However, the benefit of engaging such agencies is that they can offer expert advice on sponsorship selection; they can also actively scan for new and upcoming naming opportunities and will likely have experience in negotiating associated sponsorship deals.

When deciding between potential naming rights options, one of the most important factors for sponsors to consider is the degree of fit between their brand and the various stadia (and their resident teams) under consideration. While fit can be, to an extent, manufactured through effective activation, the examples discussed in Chapter 4 highlight how important fit is in shaping fan (and other stakeholder) reactions to sponsorship and therefore influencing the overall likelihood of success in any naming rights sponsorship deal. Thus, potential sponsors should carry out research to assess the level of fit with all potential stadia. Importantly, sponsors must recognise that fit is subjective and what a brand owner thinks represents a good fit might not be perceived in the same way by fans, consumers, or other stakeholders. Therefore, it is incumbent upon potential naming rights sponsors to carry out research with stakeholders to assess fit, rather than relying purely on internal evaluations. An example which illustrates this point is the case of English football club York City, whose Bootham Crescent stadium was renamed Kit Kat Crescent in 2005 following a naming rights deal with chocolate manufacturer Nestlé, which owns the Kit Kat brand. While on the face of it there was a strong degree of fit, with Kit Kat chocolate bars being produced in York at the time, the new name also drew some ridicule from fans (and rivals) for its comical sound. Clearly, depending on the target market of the naming rights sponsors, the extent to which negative reactions from certain stakeholder groups outweigh any positive perceptions and wider benefits will differ. This further reinforces the need for all naming rights options to be appraised individually on their own merits – a one-size-fits-all approach to assessing fit will not work. As such, an important question for potential naming rights sponsors to ask for all options under consideration is:

> *Does this naming rights sponsorship represent a good fit with our brand among all relevant stakeholder groups?*

In cases where functional and/or geographic fit between the brand and facility may be appropriate but image fit is lacking, aligning the naming rights sponsorship with the organisation's other sponsorships and activation strategies can be used to bridge this image gap. Scotiabank Arena in Toronto, Canada is one such example where image fit was created by aligning with other marketing efforts. Scotiabank does not feature an obvious functional fit with a sports stadium and, while the bank is now headquartered in Toronto, the geographic fit is not perfect since it is a national brand that was founded on the east coast of Canada, and is still formally registered as the Bank of Nova Scotia (Scotiabank is a trade name). However, Scotiabank has spent years developing its brand into 'Canada's hockey bank'; in addition to sponsorships with five of the seven Canadian-based NHL teams (including naming rights to the Scotiabank Saddledome, home of the Calgary Flames) and numerous Canadian Hockey League (elite level under-21) teams (including naming rights to the Scotiabank Centre, home of the Halifax Mooseheads, in Nova Scotia), the company sponsors Hockey Canada (the national governing body) and is the official bank of the Professional Women's Hockey Players' Association. Scotiabank also supports over one million children through minor hockey teams, and is involved in several initiatives that encourage children from diverse backgrounds to play hockey. Thus, through this long-term approach to becoming the bank/brand of hockey, any new hockey-related initiatives (such as the Scotiabank Arena naming rights) will likely be perceived as having a high fit by relevant stakeholders, particularly consumers. However, good fit alone may not be enough to convince more invested stakeholder groups, such as employees or shareholders. As such, the next question should probably be:

> *How will we integrate this naming rights sponsorship to be consistent with our overall marketing/brand strategy?*

Similar to the point above regarding how naming rights should align with an organisation's other sponsorships for fit, brands should consider being proactive in communicating with their internal stakeholders on how a naming rights sponsorship will augment the organisation's brand, as well as how it will satisfy new/existing goals and objectives within the overall marketing strategy. One key element is to reinforce how the markets impacted by the naming rights (e.g., sport fans nationally/globally, non-sport fans regionally) align with important targets for the brand. Similarly, if the naming rights sponsorship is being used as part of a new market penetration strategy, then this should be communicated in advance to internal stakeholders for validation. In terms of broader issues like CSR, how the brand sees the naming rights deal aligning with existing initiatives and brand values is another important message to communicate to internal stakeholders.

Factors to consider when deciding on a naming rights partner – the rights holder perspective

Although fit is arguably less important to the sport organisation than the sponsor brand, it still needs to be considered. The three elements of fit (functional, image, and geographic) can be assessed similarly, and many of the important factors within them are the same. However, one related factor that should be considered even more strongly on the property side is:

How much do we know about the sponsor's business?

This question speaks to the importance of research and prospecting, which applies to all sponsorships. In the case of naming rights, however, extra scrutiny should be placed on the potential sponsor's business health, values, brand image, etc., to assess the level of risk that such a partnership would entail. In addition to these salient microeconomic concerns, macroeconomic issues such as the long-term outlook for a prospective sponsoring brand's industry should also be considered (e.g., the tech bubble collapse in the early 2000s, the current shifts away from fossil fuels to renewable energy), especially given the length of most naming rights deals. Although contracts can be written to allow the property to end a deal that goes sour due to a sponsor's poor behaviour, the existing brand associations among consumers will likely remain long after the deal has been cancelled. Although a better contract could have helped the Houston Astros exit their Enron deal (mentioned in Chapter 1), the negative associations with Enron were likely to persist in stakeholder minds regardless. It is also unclear how much due diligence the Astros did when vetting Enron as a potential sponsor, but it is very likely that given the sequence of events it may have been impossible for them to forecast what happened in advance. On the other hand, controversy surrounding GEO Group had been in the public eye long before Florida Atlantic University (FAU) agreed to accept their naming rights offer (discussed in Chapter 4; Dahl, 2008). Although we cannot speak to the decision-making process from FAU, the potential for at least some public backlash could arguably have been predicted in this case. This issue also links to whether there is any risk in how a club's fans will adopt the new name more generally, which leads to the next question:

How might the deal affect our current stakeholders?

Properties should also consider the issue of complementarity between the naming sponsor and other existing sponsors. In particular, if other sponsors may have to adjust their activations to accommodate the naming sponsor, this could create a problem for the property's activation team. This issue also extends to whether or not other brands that may be sponsors in the future may be alienated based on the choice of naming partner. Although exclusivity is no longer as highly demanded by sponsors as it was in previous decades, it is still worth considering how competing brands will react.

Shifting the focus to fans, to summarise what appears elsewhere in the book (e.g., Chapter 4), fans are generally accepting of corporate names for new stadia, but are generally more hesitant (or worse) towards renaming existing stadia. The latter problem can be exacerbated if the previous name was a particularly good fit, or where there was an affectionate nickname, or songs or other traditions closely linked to the stadium name that would be less relevant with a new corporate partner (Gillooly et al., 2021). For example, despite the positive elements of the Scotiabank Arena deal that we have mentioned previously, the previous name (Air Canada Centre) was well liked in the market, exhibited good fit, and the Arena was frequently referred to by the acronym ACC (by fans and media alike). Thus, there was some negative backlash towards the Scotiabank deal, in large part due to the fact that the new name was more inconvenient to say. If the new name is not accepted by fans, a rift can be created between 'us' (the fans) and 'them' (the owners/management), which can lead to numerous negative outcomes for the property (Gillooly et al., 2021). In order to partially offset these issues, a property can explore ways to commemorate a previous stadium or venue name (e.g., applying an old name to the streets around a newly sponsored stadium or to denote parts of the venue space like a stand, and selling memorabilia which references a former stadium name), though these efforts can be tricky to implement in a genuine way (Gillooly et al., 2021).

Assuming that the property is comfortable with the deal after the previous considerations, the last question is:

What is the value of our naming rights, and should we wait to get top dollar?

Although this is technically a two-part question, the two elements are closely connected because there are only so many brands exploring the naming rights market at any one time, and relatively few available naming opportunities to choose from. As such, a market valuation approach tends to be the popular method for determining naming rights prices in practice. However, there is some research that has explored using a more asset-based valuation approach (i.e., using hedonic pricing) for naming rights sponsorships (Popp et al., 2016). This can give administrators for a given stadium or venue a more thorough understanding of how its naming rights stack up compared to other venue-based organisations. Although this research is important, it cannot be ignored that a brand's willingness to pay (WTP) arguably has more impact on naming rights prices than other sponsorships, given the uniqueness of the space/potential sponsored property involved. That being said, large brands, in particular, tend to have greater WTP to access less cluttered environments (like naming rights), especially in large markets (Jensen, 2017).

Instead of breaking down the various factors that impact naming rights values, which has been done elsewhere (we recommend readers begin with Popp et al. [2016]), we will focus more on the second half of the question about waiting for top dollar. Ultimately, the biggest naming deals continue to appear in major media markets, so properties in smaller markets should be careful not to get overconfident with their valuation. Instead, it may be best to seek a sponsor with good fit who is willing to sign a long-term deal, even if the agreed price for this is perhaps lower than hoped.

Research has suggested that sponsors are prepared to pay a premium for naming rights of new, previously unnamed stadia (Gerrard et al., 2007). Throughout time, the largest deals have been for new stadia (Scotiabank Arena, mentioned previously, is one of the few notable exceptions). Metlife Stadium in New Jersey is an interesting case in that it opened in 2010 as New Meadowlands Stadium (a reference to the area around the stadium), with Metlife not secured as a naming sponsor until 2011. The deal did turn into one of the largest in the world (exact figures have not been disclosed), and it is certainly one example of where waiting for top dollar worked. However, the Metlife case is a bit of an outlier, as it is an NFL stadium in one of the world's largest and most important sport markets. It would be unwise to suggest that such a strategy would pay off for all new stadia.

In the case of an existing stadium, there is perhaps greater flexibility in thinking about how to judge the value of naming rights. For an existing facility that is seeking its first corporate sponsored name, depending on the forecasted level of anger from fans it may make sense for the property to seek a shorter-term deal with a brand that is purely seeking high levels of awareness and is less concerned with any potential negative associations. Once the shock/anger of the stadium bearing a corporate name has worn off, perhaps after a few years, the property could seek a longer-term sponsor with better fit (which may now see the opportunity as more attractive from the fan perspective).

If a stadium already holds a corporate name with a good fit (particularly one that is well liked), then it is probably best for the property to wait for a sponsor that offers fit at a similar level, rather than taking whatever is available and risking creating a negative brand association for the property (unless the price is too good to be ignored). That said, naming rights are unique in that, as in the Metlife example, if no sponsor is secured, the stadium still needs a name. This differs from other pieces of club inventory (e.g., stands or other areas in a stadium) where a name is not often widely visible or even necessary. Although there is no direct research to inform strategy here, we posit that having a temporary team- or region-based name for a period of a year or two after a corporate name would be unlikely to significantly damage either fan perceptions or naming rights valuation. This is, therefore, a scenario where we believe properties are in the best situation to wait for the type of sponsor/deal that they want for the long term. All of the above is, of course, based on an assumption that rights holders can afford to wait. Depending on the financial precarity of a stadium and/or its incumbent teams, rights holders may have little choice but to accept the highest offer on the table. Such an approach, while recognising the financial imperatives of operating a sports stadium, does come with a health warning relating to the potential consequences (image-related and in terms of future financial value) of signing a deal with an inappropriate naming rights partner.

Length of naming rights deals and likelihood of sponsorship renewal

From both sides, a significant body of research suggests that longer-term sponsorship deals are more effective than short-term deals on a range of metrics, including brand awareness (McDonald & Karg, 2015), and fan perceptions of sponsorship fit (Olson & Thjømøe, 2011; Woisetschläger et al., 2017). As discussed in Chapter 1, stadium naming rights deals tend to be of a longer duration than other forms of sports sponsorship such as shirt or event sponsorship. In fact, research by Jensen and Head (2020) has suggested that the longer a naming rights partnership continues, the less likely the sponsor is to end the partnership. Accordingly, getting the decision of who to partner with in a naming rights deal correct from the outset seems crucial – by selecting the right partner, both sides in the deal are maximising the likelihood of the sponsorship being a success and its subsequent renewal. This type of extended relationship then bears fruit both for sponsors in terms of their brand objectives and rights holders in terms of continuity of revenue.

However, it would be naïve to assume that purely because naming rights deals tend to be longer-term initially they are automatically going to be fruitful partnerships for both parties; work will always be required on both sides to nurture such relationships. To maximise the probability of a stadium naming rights sponsor renewing at the end of their initial deal, rights holders should work with the sponsor to ensure that they are achieving their objectives. However, even where a given naming rights deal has been successful, there are occasions where a sponsor may opt not to renew, perhaps if there have been changes in corporate strategy that dictate a shift in focus or direction for the sponsor brand, or where organisations have been taken over by (or merged with) competitors. Therefore, there are no guarantees of renewal, but there are factors which can make renewal more likely.

In work on US college sport sponsorship, Jensen and Cornwell (2021) identified regional proximity of sponsor and rights holder, level of sponsorship, and business-to-business focus of the sponsor (as contrasted with a business-to-consumer focus) as factors reducing the likelihood of a partnership being dissolved. As discussed in Chapter 4, geographic fit between naming rights sponsor and rights holder can lessen fan resistance to a sponsorship. In turn, if a sponsorship is successful as a result of being well received by fans, then this may encourage naming rights sponsors to renew the deal. While Jensen and Cornwell's (2021) research looked at sponsorship of one-off post-season college football games, they identified that more prestigious levels of sponsorship may result in the reduced likelihood of a deal being ended. Therefore, given what we know about the high profile and visibility associated with stadia naming rights sponsorships, it is reasonable to assume that such deals might be more resistant to dissolution than those of a lower level. This suggests that naming rights holders should be emphasising the benefits of long-term deals and relationships to potential sponsors at the negotiation stage. In explaining the finding that sponsors pursuing business-to-business goals through their sponsorship were less likely to end the partnership, Jensen and Cornwell (2021) identify that such sponsor brands tend to appreciate that pursuit of these types of goals is a long-term endeavour. This is contrasted with technology brands as sponsors. Drawing on the work of Clark et al. (2002; 2009), Jensen and Cornwell (2021) indicate that technology brands might prefer to extract short-term value from sponsorships, meaning that the partnerships involved here may be shorter-lived. These factors are all important for rights holders to consider when approaching potential naming rights sponsors as they can shape the likelihood of nurturing a successful, long-term naming rights deal, which is something in the interests of both parties.

Conclusion

What the research presented throughout this chapter tells us is that the decision of who to partner with in a naming rights sponsorship deal is far from simple. It is evident, not only in this chapter, but throughout the whole book, that both potential sponsors and stadia rights holders should take a research-informed approach to any naming rights sponsorship decision for a given venue. This includes understanding the latest research on what naming rights sponsorship can achieve (Chapter 2), how naming rights work (Chapters 2 and 3), and gaining a full appreciation of the likely response of fans and other stakeholders (Chapter 4). In addition, both parties should thoroughly research potential naming rights partners to assess their suitability, prior to entering into any agreement.

This chapter also discussed factors which can impact on the likelihood or otherwise of a naming rights sponsorship deal being renewed. Chief among these is the extent to which the sponsorship is still contributing positively to the naming rights sponsor's objectives, meaning it is important for both sponsors and rights holders to work in partnership throughout the duration of the deal to maximise this likelihood. A range of other factors influencing renewal rates were also outlined, and an appreciation of these can help decision-makers on both sides of a naming rights partnership as a contract nears its end. One such factor is the nature of the naming rights sponsor brand. As first discussed in Chapter 1, the nature of brands engaging in naming rights sponsorship is changing, and this is one of the key future trends in naming rights to which we will turn our attention in the next chapter.

References

Clark, J. M., Cornwell, T. B., & Pruitt, S. W. (2002). Corporate stadium sponsorships, signalling theory, agency conflicts and shareholder wealth. *Journal of Advertising Research, 42*(6), 16–32. https://doi.org/10.2501/JAR. 42.6.16

Clark, J. M., Cornwell, T. B., & Pruitt, S. W. (2009). The impact of title event sponsorship announcements on shareholder wealth. *Marketing Letters, 20*(2), 169–182. https://doi.org/10.1007/s11002-008-9064-z

Dahl, J. (2008, August 5). *Private Prison Co. Again Accused of Human Rights Abuses.* https://abcnews.go.com/Blotter/story?id=5466166&page=1

Gerrard, B., Parent, M. M., & Slack, T. (2007). What drives the value of stadium naming rights? A hedonic-pricing approach to the valuation of sporting intangible assets. *International Journal of Sport Finance, 2*(1), 10–24.

Jensen, J. A. (2017). Assessing corporate demand for sponsorship: Marketing costs in the financial services industry. *Marketing Letters, 28*(2), 281–291. https://doi.org/10.1007/s11002-016-9410-5

Jensen, J. A., & Cornwell, T. B. (2021). Assessing the dissolution of horizontal marketing relationships: The case of corporate sponsorship of sport. *Journal of Business Research, 124*, 790–799. https://doi.org/10.1016/j.jbusres.2018.10.029

Jensen, J. A., & Head, D. (2020). An advancement in the study of marketing partnership longevity: analysing sport sponsorship survival. *International Journal of Sport Management and Marketing, 20*(1–2), 64–91. https://doi.org/10.1504/IJSMM.2020.109761

McDonald, H., & Karg, A. (2015). Quantifying the positive effects of sponsor level, length, prominence and relatedness on recall and residual recall rates over time. *Journal of Marketing Communications, 21*(5), 372–391. https://doi.org/10.1080/13527266.2013.778323

Olson, E. L., & Thjømøe, H. M. (2011). Explaining and articulating the fit construct in sponsorship. *Journal of Advertising, 40*(1), 57–70. https://doi.org/10.2753/JOA0091-3367400104

Popp, N., DeSchriver, T., McEvoy, C., & Diehl, M. A. (2016). A valuation analysis of corporate naming rights for collegiate sport venues. *Sport Marketing Quarterly, 25*(1), 7–20.

Woisetschläger, D. M., Backhaus, C., & Cornwell, T. B. (2017). Inferring corporate motives: How deal characteristics shape sponsorship perceptions. *Journal of Marketing, 81*(5), 121–141. https://doi.org/10.1509/jm.16.0082

6   The Future of Naming Rights Sponsorship in Sport

Throughout the book so far we have examined why brands might wish to engage in stadia naming rights sponsorship, the benefits this offers to wider stakeholders and how such partnerships can be best selected, managed and delivered, drawing on both academic research and a wealth of practical examples. In this final chapter, we turn our gaze towards the future, offering our insight into what we believe will be the key trends and directions for stadia naming rights sponsorship, both from an academic perspective and for practitioners. We discuss six key trends that we propose will be important, drawing on emerging bodies of literature and cutting-edge practices in naming rights sponsorship and beyond. The chapter will conclude with some final reflections on the current state of play in the world of naming rights and how both scholars and practitioners alike can work (hopefully together) to advance our understanding of naming rights sponsorship in the future.

The changing nature of naming rights sponsors

As mentioned in Chapter 1, we have seen brands from a number of different industries enter the naming rights space over the last four decades, with mixed results (e.g., the decline of airlines compared to the longevity of telecommunications/banks). After the tech bubble of the early 2000s, technology companies were largely absent from the naming rights market for the next two decades. With all due respect to SAP, whose successful naming rights deals date back to the mid-2000s, Amazon's Climate Pledge Arena deal may serve as a tipping point for major technology firms starting to explore naming rights more seriously. The expansion of digital technology and the Internet into most aspects of our daily lives has pushed major technology brands to become some of the largest corporations in the world (e.g., Apple, Microsoft, Alphabet (Google), Amazon, Meta (Facebook), and Nvidia are

DOI: 10.4324/9781003111849–6

all currently in the top 10 globally by market capitalisation). Thus, it is possible that, with much deeper pockets than in the early 2000s, more major technology firms could follow Amazon's lead. Several of these brands are already involved quite heavily in sports sponsorship – for example, Microsoft and Apple have their devices used by coaches and players in-game in the NFL and MLB, respectively. Between these two market leaders, along with quickly emerging companies like Netflix, PayPal, and Shopify, sport properties may have more opportunities in the future to seek sponsors within the technology space.

Linked to growth in the technology sector more broadly, at the time of writing there is an emerging trend for cryptocurrency-related companies, particularly exchange websites, getting involved in sports sponsorship (including naming rights). As outlined in Chapter 1, the Staples Center in Los Angeles was recently renamed to Crypto.com Arena in the largest naming rights deal to date (20 years, $700 million). This follows Crypto.com's competitor FTX buying naming rights to both the former American Airlines Arena in Miami and the football stadium at the University of California, Berkeley (as discussed in Chapter 3). Cryptocurrency is currently a very polarising topic; some suggest that it will fundamentally change the global economy, while others believe it is the biggest bubble in modern history. The current situation with cryptocurrency is reminiscent of the upstart technology brands that entered the naming rights space to earn legitimacy during the early 2000s, where we also saw very large deals coming from relatively new companies in an unproven industry. It will be interesting to follow in the coming years whether crypto-related companies become the biggest players in naming rights and make these deals look like shrewd business on the part of the sport properties, or if these brands (and their money) disappear as quickly as they came, similar to those technology firms at the start of the 21st century. What we do know is that the cryptocurrency companies, as well as the large technology brands mentioned above, are now truly global businesses with a presence on every continent in the world. Thus, if brands within these industries do decide to expand their naming rights portfolios, we may see shifts in both the number of global markets which they attempt to penetrate (similar to what Allianz has done), or potentially see an arms race develop for deals with the venues that are most visible on the global stage.

Authenticity in naming rights sponsorship

As identified in Chapter 4, the concept of fit has long been important in explaining sponsorship effectiveness. More recently, scholars have begun to question the continued relevance of fit as an explanatory variable for sponsorship effectiveness given the ubiquity of sponsor involvement in sport (Cornwell, 2019). The suggested alternative is perceived brand authenticity (Charlton & Cornwell, 2019; Cornwell & Kwon, 2020), defined by Morhart et al. (2015, p. 203) as 'the extent to which consumers perceive a brand to be faithful toward itself (continuity), true to its consumers (credibility), motivated by caring and responsibility (integrity), and able to support consumers in being true to themselves (symbolism)'. Given that naming rights sponsors are often seen as having more calculative motives than other sponsors (Woisetschlager et al., 2017; see Chapter 2 for a fuller discussion), we suggest that the quest for authenticity in sponsorship relationships might become increasingly relevant in the context of naming rights.

As suggested in Chapter 4, while fans can reconcile a lack of fit between a naming rights sponsor and their clubs' stadium if the financial contribution made by the sponsor is perceived as sufficient, such sponsors don't necessarily benefit from the same level of positive fan sentiment. In other words, it is a reluctant acceptance. In such cases, using the definition above, it is reasonable to surmise that fans' perceptions of the authenticity of the naming rights sponsorship may also be low as such sponsorships are perceived as lacking in the authenticity dimensions of integrity and symbolism. As consumers increasingly seek out brands which they perceive as authentic, so there is an opportunity to use naming rights sponsorship as a way of demonstrating authenticity. This may be through the naming rights themselves or through activation (Cornwell, 2019). We thus echo calls to assess the role of authenticity in sponsorship (Charlton & Cornwell, 2019; Cornwell & Kwon, 2020). Specifically, we extend such calls to suggest naming rights as a particularly ripe arena for this future research given the motives often attributed to it and the contextual factors which explain its success.

A point of particular note when it comes to naming rights sponsorships is that as the market matures, then more and more naming rights sponsorship opportunities will emerge for stadia that have possessed numerous corporate names. As discussed in Chapter 4, sports stadia can be viewed as memory places (Boyd, 2000), whereby the name represents a relationship between fans, the club, and the stadium. Changing the name of a stadium potentially disrupts this relationship and thus sponsors who are not the first to name a stadium face significant challenges in usurping previous names in consumers' memories. While memories attached to a previous stadium name can still exist, the threat posed by the new name may be lessened if fans perceive the sponsor behind it to be authentic. As such, we believe there is a real opportunity (and indeed need) for such sponsors to express their brand authenticity by selecting naming rights opportunities which, both on the surface and through appropriate activation, will offer continuity, credibility, integrity, and symbolism for their brand. We therefore advocate authenticity as an important area of focus for the future of both research and practice in naming rights sponsorship.

A commitment to sustainability through naming rights

A key contemporary trend which cannot be ignored is the need for all organisations to act in a more sustainable manner. Analysis from the PwC Sports Survey 2021 suggests that the 'majority of young fans feel sports should do more to drive positive change' (PwC, 2021). Consequently, sports organisations should be motivated to enhance their commitments to sustainable practices in order to maintain the trust of their audiences (PwC, 2021). This growing desire and need for stadia to operate sustainably presents opportunities for both stadia naming rights holders and sponsors. These opportunities could arise through careful consideration of partner selection in naming rights agreements. As discussed in Chapter 4, English football club Forest Green Rovers has a deeply ingrained commitment to sustainability, and in 2021 announced that it wanted to partner with an organisation working on environmental issues (The Stadium Business, 2021) as its new naming rights sponsor (to replace drinks brand Innocent). A deal was duly signed with Fully Charged, a YouTube channel devoted to clean energy and electric vehicles (Forest Green Rovers, 2021), with the stadium being renamed The Fully Charged New Lawn. While Forest Green Rovers has been hailed as a leader in its commitment to sustainability across its entire operation, growing fan expectations and the likelihood of increasing pressure and regulation around sustainable practices mean that many other sports clubs will face the challenge of developing their stadia to be more sustainable. Therefore, following the lead of Forest Green Rovers, we suggest that sustainability can and should play a significant role in future naming rights deals, with rights holders looking to partner with sponsors who can contribute to and augment their sustainability practices and credentials.

The PwC Sports Survey 2021 also suggests that sustainability will play an increasing role in sponsorship activation (PwC, 2021). In a sports event context, an example of such practice is the 'Tree for a Try' activation by Rugby League World Cup 2021 partner Kuehne+Nagel, whereby the logistics sponsor brand pledged to plant a tree for every try scored in the men's, women's, and wheelchair tournaments

(Kuehne+Nagel, 2021). From opportunities for showcasing sustainable products in stadia (or as part of their construction) through to facilitating initiatives around waste, energy consumption, water usage, or sustainable transport, there is a real opportunity (and, given fans' expectations, a real business imperative) for naming rights sponsors to work with stadia rights holders to put sustainability at the heart of their activations.

Naming rights as part of larger sponsorship packages

As mentioned throughout the book, naming rights sponsors are more engaged than ever with activation to complement their naming rights sponsorships, as well as using naming rights as elements within broader campaigns or branding strategies. For example, it was discussed in Chapter 5 how Scotiabank has used its naming rights of arenas in Toronto, Calgary, and Halifax as centrepieces in its much broader endeavour to become 'Canada's hockey bank' at virtually all levels of the sport pyramid (grassroots, professional, national federation, etc.). Allianz appears to be working towards something similar with a more global approach in football, naming stadia in seven different countries on four continents where professional teams play. Emirates similarly crosses continents with its deals in the UK and South Africa. We expect that other organisations will follow suit in conceptualising naming rights opportunities as one key part of their integrated national or global branding strategies.

This begs the question of whether naming rights have evolved from a special type of standalone sponsorship to be a passive form of activation. Unlike a regular sponsorship deal where rights are secured and then activation is added afterwards (at additional cost), in naming rights the facility name is the centrepiece of the deal from the start. However, even with standard sponsorships, much of the conversation about activation is now being had up front and those ideas are built into the deal from the beginning. Historically when a naming rights deal ended, so did the relationship between brand and property, whereas activations within a regular sponsorship (even signage) could be replaced or altered at virtually any time. Now, however, we are seeing examples of where former naming rights partners are staying on as team sponsors even after not renewing their naming deal (e.g., Air Canada with the Toronto Raptors). In the future, therefore, we propose that naming rights may become better conceptualised as a form of passive activation, rather than a standalone or 'special' type of sponsorship. This represents a fairly dramatic shift in thinking, particularly for those that do not agree that passive forms of activation should be called activation at all. However, given the structure of recent exemplar deals and brands' motivations behind them, we believe that it is time for both academics and practitioners to begin to think of naming rights as a major component of sponsorship, rather than a type of sponsorship itself.

Moving beyond the premier level of venues

Naming rights sponsorship at the premier levels of sport (e.g., globally visible professional sport) has generally legitimised corporate naming in most developed countries. As that premier level has become increasingly saturated, there is more opportunity for properties further down the sport pyramid to secure naming rights partners. As mentioned in Chapter 1, since naming rights gained acceptance on the grandest scale, we are now seeing more community-level or regional venues who see the potential of naming rights and are also able to find interested partners. This is occurring mainly within North America, but also in a few other regions and countries around the world (particularly Western Europe). Minor league sport in North America (which is professional sport, but with mainly community-/regional-level exposure) is becoming a particularly popular sport context for naming rights. Within this space, most of the naming sponsors are smaller brands (e.g., regional banks), but some large corporations have also signed deals for these smaller professional facilities (e.g., Coca-Cola, TD Bank, Toyota).

Naming rights have also begun to gain traction with community-level, amateur sport facilities, with two examples being the Northern Community Centre in Sault Ste. Marie, Canada, which is sponsored by Northern Credit Union, and the Capri Pizzeria Recreation Complex in Windsor, Canada (the latter of which was mentioned in Chapter 1). These types of facilities create opportunities for smaller, local businesses to engage in naming rights sponsorship, and are a way for brands (both small and large) to show that they are making an investment in those communities where they do business. Although the practice of naming school facilities tends to be more contentious, with the growth in that sector within the USA, it could be that school facilities globally will start to see an uptick in naming rights interest from brands.

In addition to sport sector diversification, there is considerable opportunity to grow naming rights in less developed sporting countries. We consider fewer than ten countries to currently be 'mature' naming rights markets (including Canada, Germany, Japan, Sweden, the UK, and the USA). Among the most developed sporting countries, France, Spain, Italy, and Mexico have relatively few naming rights deals compared to countries with similar populations and established sport systems. In terms of more emerging markets, we are beginning to see an increase in naming rights in Brazil, Russia, and Turkey, while India and China, by far the two largest countries in the world by population, remain virtually untapped. As sport continues to globalise, and the economies of these emerging markets continue to see expansion in the middle classes, more stadia around the world will become attractive naming opportunities, particularly for global brands seeking to penetrate/grow in such markets (e.g., potentially the large global technology brands mentioned above). These trends thus give optimism for the future of naming rights sponsorship beyond its current scale, scope, and form.

Naming virtual spaces

Looking beyond traditional, physical sports stadia, a trend that might go further in extending naming rights beyond their current scope is the use of augmented reality (AR) and virtual reality (VR) technologies, opening up the prospect of virtual stadia for which naming rights could be sold. Until recently, the most that sports organisations leveraged AR or VR technologies was with virtual stadium tours on their websites. However, over the last few years, and perhaps accelerated by the Covid-19 pandemic, virtual stadia are starting to appear; for example, the Canadian Premier League Island Games 2020 were played in a simple facility that did not have a traditional stadium environment, so one was created for the broadcast (including a virtual video board that showed fan-submitted photos on the screen; Canadian Premier League, 2020). In other cases, sports organisations are looking to create virtual versions of their current stadia to offer a broader range of digital fan experiences. For example, Manchester City has taken a step into the metaverse, working with Sony to create its own virtual version of the Etihad stadium (Shumba, 2021). These digital spaces might again offer up new opportunities for naming rights sponsorship, with a virtual stadium having its own naming rights partner. Going a step further, rights holders could offer naming rights for virtual stadia (or spaces within these virtual stadia) to different brands in different markets, thus broadening revenue streams.

Beyond the stadium itself, AR and VR technologies present opportunities for the creation of a wide range of virtual spaces, such as fan cafes, virtual training facilities, or fan zones, where fans can interact and engage with their favourite sports team or players. In a similar way to virtual stadia, naming rights to these virtual spaces (and associated activation opportunities) could be offered to potential sponsor brands seeking ways of engaging with global audiences. A specific opportunity in this regard might be the creation of virtual e-sports venues, such as Liquid+ (Gardner, 2021). Many professional sports clubs already have e-sports teams, so creating dedicated virtual e-sports venues for their matches (either that mimic the physical stadium or not) could facilitate a greater connection between the physical and e-sports teams. Major brands are showing increasing interest in e-sports partnerships, so the naming rights associated with these virtual spaces might offer brands another means of engaging with e-sports audiences. Such a move may also appeal to technology brands wanting naming rights in a digital space more congruent with their brand values. The extent to which naming rights opportunities for virtual stadia will come to fruition clearly depends on the continued growth, development and adoption of AR, VR, and associated technologies, but what this trend highlights is a real opportunity for sponsors and rights holders to think beyond the physical in both the selling and activation of naming rights going forward.

Conclusion

This chapter has explored six key trends that we believe to be salient for the future of naming rights sponsorship. In doing so, our aim was to outline an agenda for both practice and academic research in the field. Clearly, only time will tell as to the quality of our predictions regarding the impact of these trends within naming rights. However, what this chapter does demonstrate is cause to be optimistic about naming rights, in whatever form they may take going forward.

Throughout its history, naming rights sponsorship has pushed boundaries, whether that be in the financial sums involved, the way in which both brand and rights holder objectives have evolved, or through use of innovative activation techniques. As with all aspects of marketing activity, the world of naming rights sponsorship cannot afford to stand still and we sincerely hope that this book has, in some way, contributed to furthering understanding of not only how naming rights are done today, but also how they can be done in the future. In particular, reprising a discussion from Chapter 5, the role of research will become increasingly important as stadia naming rights holders and potential sponsors grapple with current and emergent trends. While much academic research has been done in the area of naming rights, as we have cited throughout this book, the knowledge base is still far from robust, and more work is needed. In particular, much of the current research is observational and/or performed by academics on their own without any industry involvement or partnerships. Such collaboration will be important in continuing to grow the knowledge base in this niche area of the sponsorship field. It is our hope, therefore, that practitioners and academics might seek to work more closely together to continue to advance our understanding of what best practice in naming rights sponsorship might look like.

References

Boyd, J. (2000). Selling home: Corporate stadium names and the destruction of commemoration. *Journal of Applied Communication Research, 28*(4), 330–346. https://doi.org/10.1080/00909880009365580

Canadian Premier League. (2020). *Canadian Premier League unveils Canadian-First Virtual Stadium for 2020 Island Games.* https://canpl.ca/article/canadian-premier-league-unveils-canadian-first-virtual-stadium-for-2020-island-games

Charlton, A. B., & Cornwell, T. B. (2019). Authenticity in horizontal marketing partnerships: A better measure of brand compatibility. *Journal of Business Research, 100*, 279–298. https://doi.org/10.1016/j.jbusres.2019.03.054

Cornwell, T. B. (2019). Less "sponsorship as advertising" and more sponsorship-linked marketing as authentic engagement. *Journal of Advertising, 48*(1), 49–60. https://doi.org/10.1080/00913367.2019.1588809

Cornwell, T. B., & Kwon, Y. (2020). Sponsorship-linked marketing: Research surpluses and shortages. *Journal of the Academy of Marketing Science, 48*(4), 607–629. https://doi.org/10.1007/s11747-019-00654-w

Forest Green Rovers. (2021). *Fully Charged.* https://www.fgr.co.uk/partners/fully-charged

Gardner, M. (2021, January 26). *Team Liquid Unveils Radical Esports 'Virtual Stadium' For 2021.* https://www.forbes.com/sites/mattgardner1/2021/01/26/team-liquid-unveils-radical-virtual-stadium-esports-experience-for-2021/?sh=5b6ca8829522

Kuehne+Nagel. (2021, June 4). *Kuehne+Nagel announce 'Tree for a Try' at Rugby League World Cup 2021.* https://uk.kuehne-nagel.com/-/news/rlwc-tree-for-a-try

Morhart, F., Malär, L., Guèvremont, A., Girardin, F., & Grohmann, B. (2015). Brand authenticity: An integrative framework and measurement scale. *Journal of Consumer Psychology, 25*(2), 200–218. https://doi.org/10.1016/j.jcps.2014.11.006

PwC. (2021). *Sports Industry: Ready for Recovery? PwC's Sports Survey 2021.* https://www.pwc.ch/en/insights/sport/sports-survey-2021.html

Shumba, C. (2021, December 1). *Manchester City has Teamed Up with Sony to Create a Metaverse Out of a Virtual Version of Its Soccer Stadium.* https://markets.businessinsider.com/news/currencies/metaverse-investing-crypto-sport-manchester-city-sony-nft-sandbox-decentraland-2021-12

The Stadium Business. (2021, June 22). *Forest Green Launches Contest for Eco-Friendly Stadium Sponsor.* https://www.thestadiumbusiness.com/2021/06/22/forest-green-launches-contest-for-eco-friendly-stadium-sponsor/

Woisetschläger, D. M., Backhaus, C., & Cornwell, T. B. (2017). Inferring corporate motives: How deal characteristics shape sponsorship perceptions. *Journal of Marketing, 81*(5), 121–141. https://doi.org/10.1509/jm.16.0082

Index

Note: Page numbers followed by "n" denote endnotes.

For Product Safety Concerns and Information please contact our EU
representative GPSR@taylorandfrancis.com Taylor & Francis Verlag GmbH,
Kaufingerstraße 24, 80331 München, Germany

Printed and bound by CPI Group (UK) Ltd, Croydon, CR0 4YY

28/01/2026

02044219-0001